HEAVEN

HEAVEN

Dwight L. Moody

MOODY PRESS

CHICAGO

Originally published in
1880 and 1884 by Fleming Revell,
now a division of Baker Books

Updated edition 1995 by
THE MOODY BIBLE INSTITUTE
OF CHICAGO

Scripture quotations, unless indicated otherwise, are tak-
en from the King James Version.

ISBN: 0-8024-5446-1

3 5 7 9 10 8 6 4

Printed in the United States of America

CONTENTS

EDITORIAL PREFACE

When one is young he seldom has much thought of heaven, but such thoughts do come more frequently as the years roll on.

Mr. Moody found both comfort and edification in looking "with increasing faith to the fairest of fair cities in the Better Land"—the Home of our Redeemer and, as His blood-bought children, our Home also.

There was a leading preacher of whom Mr. Moody spoke, and whose testimony impressed him when he said that as a boy he thought of heaven as a great shining city, with vast walls and domes and spires, and with nobody in it except white angels, who were strangers to him. By and by his little brother died, and he thought of a great city with walls and domes and spires, and a group of cold, unknown angels, and one little fellow that he was acquainted with. He was the only one that he knew in that country. Then another brother died, and there were two that he knew. Then his acquaintances began to die, and the number continually grew. But it was not until he had sent one of his little children back to God that he began to think he had a little interest there. A second, a third, a

fourth went, and by that time he had so many acquaintances in heaven that he did not see any
more walls and domes and spires. He began to
think of the residents of the Celestial City. Then so
many of his acquaintances went there, that it sometimes seemed that he knew more in heaven than
he did on earth.

HEAVEN
Its Hope

THE HOME OF THE SOUL

That unchangeable home is for you and for me,
  Where Jesus of Nazareth stands;
The King of all kingdoms forever is He,
  And He holdeth our crowns in His hands.

Oh, how sweet it will be in that beautiful land,
  So free from all sorrow and pain;
With songs on our lips and with harps in our hands
  To meet one another again.

1
Its Hope

*We give thanks to God and the Father of our
Lord Jesus Christ . . . for the hope which is laid
up for you in heaven.*   Colossians 1:3, 5

A great many persons imagine that anything said
about heaven is only a matter of speculation. They
talk about heaven much as they would about the
air. Now there would not have been so much in
Scripture on this subject if God had wanted to
leave the human race in darkness about it. "All
scripture," we are told, "is given by inspiration of
God, and is profitable for doctrine, for reproof, for
correction, for instruction in righteousness, that
the man of God may be perfect, throughly fur-
nished unto all good works" 2 Timothy 3:16–17.

What the Bible says about heaven is just as true
as what it says about everything else. The Bible is
inspired. What we are taught about heaven could
not have come to us in any other way than by inspiration. No one knew anything about it but God,
and so if we want to find out anything about it we
have to turn to His Word. Dr. Hodge, of Prince-
ton, said that the best evidence of the Bible being
the Word of God is to be found between its own
two covers. It proves itself. In this respect it is like

Christ, whose character proclaimed the divinity of His person. Christ showed Himself more than man by what He did. The Bible shows itself more than a human book by what it says.

It is not, however, because the Bible is *written* with more than human skill, far surpassing Shakespeare or any other human author, and that its knowledge of character and the eloquence it contains are beyond the powers of man, that we believe it to be inspired. Men's ideas differ about the extent to which human skill can be carried, but the reason why we believe the Bible to be inspired is so simple that the humblest child of God can comprehend it.

If the proof of its divine origin lay in its wisdom alone, a simple and uneducated man might not be able to believe it. We believe it is inspired because there is nothing in it that could *not* have come from God. God is wise, and God is good. There is nothing in the Bible that is not wise, and there is nothing in it that is not good. If the Bible had anything in it that was opposed to reason, or to our sense of right, then, perhaps, we might think that it was like all the books in the world that are written merely by men.

Books that are only human, like merely human lives, have in them a great deal that is foolish and a great deal that is wrong. The life of Christ alone was perfect, being both human and divine. Not one of the other volumes, such as the Koran, that claims divinity of origin agrees with common sense. There is nothing at all in the Bible that does not conform to common sense. What it tells us about the world having been destroyed by a deluge and Noah and his family alone being saved is no more wonderful than what is taught in the schools, that all of the earth we see now, and everything upon it, came out of a ball of fire. It is a great deal easier to believe that man was made after the image of God than to believe, as some young men and women are being taught now, that he is the offspring of a monkey.

Like all the other wonderful works of God, this Book bears the the sure stamp of its Author. It is like Him. Though man plants the seeds, God makes the flowers, and they are perfect and beautiful like Himself. Men wrote what is in the Bible, but the work is God's. As a rule, the more refined people are, the more they love the Bible. Fondness for flowers tends to refine people, and the love of the Bible makes them better.

All that is in the Bible about God, about man, about redemption, and about a future state agrees with our own ideas of right, with our reasonable fears, and with our personal experiences. All the historical events are described in the way that we know the world had of looking at them when they were written. What the Bible tells about heaven is not half so strange as what Professor Proctor told of the hosts of stars that are beyond the range of any ordinary telescope; and yet people very often think that science is all fact and that religion is only fancy. A great many persons think that Jupiter and many more of the stars around us are inhabited but cannot bring themselves to believe that there is beyond this earth a life for immortal souls. The true Christian puts faith before reason and believes that reason always goes wrong when faith is set aside. If people would but read their Bible more and study what there is to be found there about heaven, they would not be as worldly-minded as they are. They would not have their hearts set upon things down here, but would seek the imperishable things above.

Earth, the Home of Sin

It seems perfectly reasonable that God should have given us a glimpse of the future, for we are constantly losing some of our friends by death, and the first thought that comes to us is "Where have they gone?" When loved ones are taken away from us, how that thought comes up before us! How we wonder if we will ever see them again, and where and when it will be! Then it is that we turn to this blessed Book, for there is no other book in all the world that can give us the slightest comfort; no other book that can tell us where the loved ones have gone.

Not long ago I met an old friend, and as I took him by the hand and asked after his family, the tears came trickling down his cheeks as he said:

"I haven't any now."

"What," I said, "is your wife dead?"

"Yes, sir."

"And all your children, too?"

"Yes, all gone," he said, "and I am left here desolate and alone."

Would anyone take from that man the hope that he will meet his dear ones again? Would anyone persuade him that there is not a future where the lost will be found? No, we need not forget our dear loved ones; but we may cling forever to the enduring hope that there will be a time when we can meet unfettered and be blessed in that land of everlasting suns, where the soul drinks from the living streams of love that roll by God's high throne.

In our inmost hearts there are none of us but have questionings of the future.

> Tell me, my secret soul,
>   O tell me, Hope and Faith,
> Is there no resting-place
>   From sorrow, sin and death?
> Is there no happy spot
>   Where mortals may be blest,
> Where grief may find a balm,
>   And weariness a rest?
> Faith, Hope and Love—best boons to mortals given—
> Waved their bright wings, and whispered:
>   Yes, in heaven!

There are men who say that there is no heaven. I was once talking with a man who said he thought there was nothing to justify us in believing in any other heaven than that we know here on earth. If this is heaven, it is a very strange one —this world of sickness, sorrow, and sin. I pity from the depths of my heart the man or woman who has that idea.

This world that some think is heaven is the home of sin, a hospital of sorrow, a place that has nothing in it to satisfy the soul. Men go all over it and then want to get out of it. The more men see of the world the less they think of it. People soon grow tired of the best pleasures it has to offer.

Someone has said that the world is a stormy sea whose every wave is strewed with the wrecks of mortals that perish in it. Every time we breathe someone is dying. We all know that we are going to stay here but a very little while. Our life is but a vapor. It is only a shadow.

"We meet one another," as someone has said, "salute one another, pass on and are gone." And another has said: "It is just an inch of time, and then eternal ages roll on"; and it seems to me that it is perfectly reasonable that we should study this Book to find out where we are going and where our friends are who have gone on before. The longest time man has to live has no more proportion to eternity than a drop of dew has to the ocean.

Cities of the Past

Look at the cities of the past. There is Babylon. It is said to have been founded by a queen named Semiramis, who had two millions of men at work for years building it. Is is nothing but dust now. Nearly a thousand years ago, a historian wrote that the ruins of Nebuchadnezzar's palace were still standing, but men were afraid to go near them because they were full of scorpions and snakes. That is the sort of ruin that greatness often comes to in our own day. Nineveh is gone. Its towers and bastions have fallen. The traveler who tries to see Carthage cannot find much of it. Corinth, once the seat of luxury and art, is only a shapeless mass. Ephesus, long the metropolis of Asia, the Paris of that day, was crowded with buildings as large as the capitol at Washington. I am told it looks more like a neglected graveyard now than anything else.

Granada, once so grand, with its twelve gates and towers, is now in decay. The Alhambra, the palace of the Mohammedan kings, was situated there. Little pieces of the once grand and beautiful cities of Herculanaeum and Pompeii are now being sold in the shops for relics. Jerusalem, once the joy of the whole earth, is but a shadow of its former self. Thebes, for thousands of years, up almost to the coming of Christ, among the largest and wealthiest cities of the world, is now a mass of decay. But little of ancient Athens and many more of the proud cities of olden times remain to tell the story of their downfall. God drives His plowshare through cities, and they are upheaved like furrows in the field. "Behold," says Isaiah, "the nations are as a drop of a bucket, and are counted as the small dust of the balance; behold, He taketh up the isles as a very little thing. . . . All nations before him are as nothing; and they are counted to him less than nothing, and vanity" (40:15, 17).

See how Antioch has fallen. When Paul preached there, it was a superb metropolis. A wide street over three miles long, stretching across the entire city, was ornamented with rows of columns and covered galleries, and at every corner stood carved statues to commemorate their great men, whose names even we have never heard. These men are never heard of now, but the poor preaching tentmaker who entered its portals stands out as the grandest character in history. The finest specimens of Grecian art decorated the shrines of the temples, and the baths and the aqueducts were such as are never approached in elegance now. Men then, as now, were seeking honor, wealth, and renown, and enshrining their names and records in perishable clay.

Within the walls of Antioch, we are told, were enclosed hills over seven hundred feet high, and rocky precipices and deep ravines gave a wild and picturesque character to the place of which no modern city affords an example. These heights were fortified in a marvelous manner, which gave to them strange and startling effects. The vast population of this brilliant city, combining all the art and cultivation of Greece with the levity, the luxury, and the superstition of Asia, was as intent on pleasure as the population of any of our great cities are today. The citizens had their shows, their games, their races and dancers; their sorcerers, puzzlers, buffoons, and miracle-workers; and the people sought constantly in the theaters and processions for something to stimulate and gratify the most corrupt desires of human nature. This is pretty much what we find the masses of the people in our great cities doing now.

Antioch was even worse than Athens, for the so-called worship they indulged in was not only idolatrous, but had mixed up with it the grossest passions to which man descends. It was here that Paul came to preach the glad tidings of the Gospel of Christ; it was here that the disciples were first called Christians, as a nickname, all followers of Christ before that time having been called "saints" or "brethren." As has been well said, out of that spring at Antioch a mighty stream has flowed to water the world. Astarte, the "Queen of Heaven," whom they worshiped, Diana, Apollo, the Pharisee and Sadducee are no more, but the despised Christians yet live. Yet that heathen city, which would not take Christianity to its heart and keep it, fell. Cities that have not the restraining influences of Christianity well established in them seldom do amount to much in the long run. They grow dim in the light of ages. Few of our great cities in this country are a hundred years old as yet. For nearly a thousand years this city prospered; yet it fell.

Going to Emigrate

I do not think that it is wrong for us to think and talk about heaven. I like to locate heaven and find out all I can about it. I expect to live there through all eternity. If I were going to dwell in any place in this country, if I were going to make it my home, I would want to inquire about the place, about its climate, about the neighbors I would have, about everything, in fact, that I could learn concerning it. If any of you were going to emigrate, that would be the way you would feel. Well, we are all going to emigrate in a very little while to a country that is very far away. We are going to spend eternity in another world, a grand and glorious world where God reigns. Is it not natural, then, that we should look and listen and try to find out who is already there, and what is the route to take?

Soon after I was converted, an infidel asked me one day why I look *up* when I prayed. He said that heaven was no more above us than below us; that heaven was everywhere. Well, I was greatly bewildered, and the next time I prayed, it seemed almost as if I was praying into the air. Since then I have become better acquainted with the Bible, and I have come to see that heaven is above us; that it is upward, and not downward. The Spirit of God is everywhere, but God is in heaven, and heaven is above our heads. It does not matter what part of the globe we may stand upon, heaven is above us.

In the seventeenth chapter of Genesis it says that God went *up* from Abraham; and in the third chapter of John, that the Son of Man came *down* from heaven. So, also, in the first chapter of Acts we find that Christ went up into heaven (not down) and a cloud received him out of sight. Thus we see heaven is up. The very arrangement of the firmament about the earth declares the seat of God's glory to be above us. Job says: "Let not God regard it from *above*" (Job 3:4). Again, in Deuteronomy, we find, "Who shall go *up* for us to heaven?" (30:12). Thus, all through Scripture we find that we are given the location of heaven as upward and beyond the firmament. This firmament, with its many bright worlds scattered through, is so vast that heaven must be an extensive realm. Yet this need not surprise us. It is not for shortsighted man to inquire why God made heaven so extensive that its lights along the way can be seen from any part or side of this little world.

In Jeremiah 51:15, we are told: "He hath made the earth by his power, he hath established the world by his wisdom, and hath stretched out the heaven by his understanding." Yet, how little we really know of that power, or wisdom, or understanding! As we read in Job: "Lo, these are parts of his ways: but how little a portion is heard of Him? But the thunder of his power who can understand?" (26:14).

This is the word of God. As we find in the forty-second chapter of Isaiah: "Thus saith God the Lord, he that created the heavens, and stretched them out; he that spread forth the earth, and that which cometh out of it; he that giveth bread unto the people upon it, and spirit to them that walk within" (v. 5).

The discernment of God's power, the messages of heaven, do not always come in great things. We read in the nineteenth chapter of the first book of Kings:

> And behold, the Lord passed by, and a great and strong wind rent the mountains, and brake in pieces the rocks before the Lord; but the Lord was not in the wind: and after the wind an earthquake; but the Lord was not in the earthquake: and after the earthquake a fire; but the Lord was not in the fire: and after the fire a still small voice. (vv. 11–12)

It is a still small voice that God speaks to His children. Some people are trying to find out just how far heaven is away. There is one thing we know about it; that is, that it is not so far away but that God can hear us when we pray. I do not believe there has ever been a tear shed for sin since Adam's fall in Eden to the present time, but God has witnessed it. He is not too far from earth for us to go to Him; and if there is a sigh that comes from a burdened heart today, God will hear that sigh. If there is a cry coming up from a heart broken on account of sin, God will hear that cry. He is not so far away, heaven is not so far away, as to be inaccessible to the smallest child. In the seventh chapter of 2 Chronicles we read:

> If my people, which are called by my name, shall humble themselves, and pray, and seek my face, and turn from their wicked ways; then will I hear from heaven, and will forgive them their sin, and will heal their land. (v. 14)

When I was in Dublin, they were telling me about a father who had lost a little boy. This father had not thought about the future, he had been so entirely taken up with this world and its affairs; but when that little boy, his only child, died, that father's heart was broken, and every night when he returned from work he might be found in his room with his candle and his Bible hunting up all that he could find there about heaven. Someone asked him what he was doing, and he said he was trying to find out where his child had gone, and I think he was a reasonable man.

I supposed no one will ever read this page who has not dear ones that are gone. Shall we close this Book today, or shall we look into it to try to find where the loved ones are? I was reading, some time ago, an account of a father, a minister, who had lost a child. He had gone to a great many funerals, offering comfort to others in sorrow, but now the iron had entered his own soul, and a brother minister had come to officiate and preach the funeral sermon; and after this minister had finished speaking, the father got up, and standing at the head of the coffin, said that a few years ago, when he had first come into that parish, as he used to look over the river he took no interest in the people over there, because they were all strangers to him and there were none over there that belonged to his parish.

But, he said, a few years ago a young man came into his home and married his daughter, and she went over the river to live, and when his child went over there, he became suddenly interested in the inhabitants, and every morning as he arose he would look out of the window across the river to her home. "But now," said he, "another child has been taken. She has gone over another river, and heaven seems dearer and nearer to me now than it ever has before."

My friends, let us believe this good old Book, be confident that heaven is not a myth, and be prepared to follow the dear ones who have gone before. Thus, and thus alone, can we find the peace we seek for.

Seeking a Better Country

What has been, and is now, one of the strongest feelings in the human heart? Is it not to find some better place, some lovelier spot, than we have now? It is for this that men are seeking everywhere; and they can have it if they will; but instead of looking down, they must look *up* to find it. As men grow in knowledge, they vie with each other more and more in making their homes attractive; but the brightest home on earth is but a barn compared with the mansion in the skies.

What is it that we look for at the decline and close of life? Is it not some sheltered place, some quiet spot, where, if we cannot have constant rest, we may at least have a foretaste of the rest that is to be? What was it that led Columbus, not knowing what would be his fate, across the unsailed western seas, if it were not the hope of finding a better country? This it was that sustained the hearts of the Pilgrim Fathers, driven from their native land by persecution, as they faced an ironbound, savage coast, with an unexplored territory beyond. They were cheered and upheld by the hope of reaching a free and fruitful country, where they could be at rest and worship God in peace.

Somewhat similar is the Christian's hope of heaven, only it is not an undiscovered country and its attractions cannot be compared with anything we know on earth. Perhaps nothing but the shortness of our range of sight keeps us from seeing the celestial gates all open to us, and nothing but the deafness of our ears prevents our hearing the joyful ringing of the bells of heaven. There are constant sounds around us that we cannot hear, and the sky is studded with bright worlds that our eyes have never seen. Little as we know about this bright and radiant land, there are glimpses of its beauty that come to us now and then.

> We may not know how sweet its balmy air,
>   How bright and fair its flowers;
> We may not hear the songs that echo there,
>   Through these enchanted bowers.
>
> The city's shining towers we may not see
>   With our dim earthly vision,
> For Death, the silent warder, keeps the key
>   That opes the gates Elysian.

But sometimes when adown the western sky
  A fiery sunset lingers,
Its golden gate swings inward noiselessly,
  Unlocked by unseen fingers.

And while they stand a moment half ajar,
  Gleams from the inner glory
Stream brightly through the azure vault afar,
  And half reveal the story.

It is said by travelers that in climbing the Alps the houses of far distant villages can be seen with great distinctness, so that sometimes the number of panes of glass in a church window can be counted. The distance looks so short that the place to which the traveler is journeying appears almost at hand, but after hours and hours of climbing it seems no nearer yet. This is because of the clearness of the atmosphere. By perseverance, however, the place is reached at last, and the tired traveler finds rest. So sometimes we dwell in high altitudes of grace; heaven seems very near, and the hills of Beulah are in full view. At other times the clouds and fogs caused by suffering and sin cut off our sight. We are just as near heaven in the one case as we are in the other, and we are just as sure of gaining it if we only keep in the path that Christ has pointed out.

I have read that on the shores of the Adriatic sea the wives of fishermen, whose husbands have gone far out upon the deep, are in the habit of going down to the seashore at night and singing with their sweet voices the first verse of some beautiful hymn. After they have sung it they listen until they hear brought on the wind, across the sea, the second verse sung by their brave husbands as they are tossed by the gale—and both are happy. Perhaps, if we would listen, we too might hear on this storm-tossed world of ours some sound, some whisper, borne from afar to tell us there is a heaven which is our home; and when we sing our hymns upon the shores of the earth, perhaps we may hear their sweet echoes breaking in music upon the sands of time and cheering the hearts of those who are pilgrims and strangers along the way. Yes, we need to look up—out, beyond this low earth, and to build higher in our thoughts and actions, even here!

You know, when a man is going up in a balloon, he takes in sand as ballast, and when he wants to mount a little higher, he throws out some of it, and then he will mount a little higher; he throws out a little more ballast, and he mounts still higher; and the more he throws out the higher he gets. And so the more we have to throw out of the things of this world the nearer we get to God. Let go of them; let us not set our hearts and affections on them but do what the Master tells us—lay up for ourselves treasures in heaven.

In England I was told of a lady who had been bedridden for years. She was one of those saints whom God polishes up for the kingdom; for I believe there are many saints in this world whom we never hear about. We never see their names heralded through the press; they live very near the Master; they live very near heaven; and I think it takes a great deal more grace to suffer God's will than it does to do it; and if a person lies on a bed of sickness, and suffers cheerfully, it is just as acceptable to God as if they went out and worked in His vineyard.

Now this lady was one of those saints. She said that for a long time she used to have a great deal of pleasure in watching a bird that came to make its nest near her window. One year it came to make its nest, and it began to build so low down she was afraid something would happen to the young; and every day that she saw that bird busy at work making its nest, she kept saying, "O bird, build higher!" She could see that the bird was likely to come to grief and disappointment. At last the bird got its nest done and laid its eggs and hatched its young. And every morning the lady looked out to see if the nest was there, and she saw the old bird bringing food for the little ones, and she took a great deal of pleasure looking at it.

But one morning she awoke, looked out, and she saw nothing but feathers scattered all around, and she said: "Ah, the cat has got the old bird and all her young." It would have been a kindness to have torn that nest down. That is what God does for us very often—just snatches things away before it is too late. Now, I think that is what we want to say to professing Christians—if you build for time you will be disappointed. God says: Build up yonder. It is a good deal better to have life with Christ in God than anywhere else. I would rather have my life hid with Christ in God than be in Eden as Adam was. Adam might have remained in paradise for sixteen thousand years, and then fallen, but if our life is hid in Christ, how safe!

THOUGHTS OF HOME

O Lord, 'twas Thine to labor and wear the thorns for
  me;
Thou sharest all my sorrows; Thou knowest what
  'twill be
To see the Father's glory, to hear Thy welcome there,
Where never cross or burden remains for us to bear.

I seem to pace the glittering street, and hear the
  harps of gold,
The echo of the new song that never groweth old;
I hear Thy praise, Lord Jesus, my Life, my Lord, my
  King,
Until my worn heart pineth the strains of heaven to
  sing.

Safe in the better country my loved ones I shall find,
And some in that bright multitude I feared were left
  behind;
Then loud shall sound our praises within the jasper
  wall,
As cherubim and seraphim before the Holiest fall.

With folded wings, expectant, the angel bands will
  come
To listen to the tale of grace that wooed the children
  home;
And sitting at Thy feet, Lord, my joyful lips shall tell
How much He hath forgiven, who "doeth all things
  well."

Thou blessed Spirit, cheering this valley land for me
With glimpses of the glory of that which soon shall
  be;

Each harpstring, dull and broken, Thy gentle breath
    awaits;
Then let me sing of Jesus up to the golden gates.

Anna Shipton

HEAVEN
Its Inhabitants

A LITTLE WAY

A little way! I know it is not far
To that dear home where my beloved are;
And still my heart sits, like a bird, upon
The empty nest, and mourns its treasures gone,
  Plumed for their flight,
  And vanished quite.
Ah me! Where is the comfort? Though I say
They have but journeyed on a little way.

A little way! At times they seem so near,
Their voices even murmur in my ear,
To all my duties loving presence lend,
And with sweet ministry my steps attend.
'Twas here we met and parted company;
Why should their gain be such a grief to me?
  This sense of loss!
  This heavy cross!
Dear Savior, take the burden off, I pray,
And show me heaven is but—a little way.

A little way? The sentence I repeat,
Hoping and longing to extract some sweet
To mingle with the bitter; from Thy hand
I take the cup I cannot understand,
And in my weakness give myself to Thee.
Although it seems so very, very far
To that dear home where my beloved are,
  I know, I know,
  It is *not* so;
Oh, give me faith to believe it when I say
That they are gone—gone but a little way.

                                    —Anonymous

2

Its Inhabitants

The inhabitant shall not say, I am sick: the people that dwell therein shall be forgiven their iniquity.   Isaiah 33:24

The society of heaven will be select. No one who studies Scripture can doubt that. There are a good many kinds of aristocracy in this world, but the aristocracy of heaven will be the aristocracy of holiness. The humblest believer on earth will be an aristocrat there. It says in the fifty-seventh chapter of Isaiah: "For thus saith the high and lofty One that inhabiteth eternity, whose name is Holy; I dwell in the high and holy place, with him also that is of a contrite and humble spirit" (v. 15). Now what could be plainer than that? No one who is not of a contrite and humble spirit will dwell with God in His high and holy place.

If there is anything that ought to make heaven near to Christians, it is knowing that God and all their loved ones will be there. What is it that makes home so attractive? Is it because we have a beautiful home? Is it because we have beautiful lawns? Is is because we have beautiful trees around us? Is it because we have beautiful paintings upon the walls inside? Is it because we have beautiful furniture? Is that all that makes homes so attractive and beautiful? Nay, it is the loved ones in it; it is the loved ones there.

I remember after being away from home some time, I went back to see my honored mother, and I thought in going back I would take her by surprise and steal in unexpectedly upon her, but when I found she had gone away, the old place didn't seem like home at all. I went into one room and then into another, and all through the house, but I could not find that loved mother, and I asked some member of the family, "Where is Mother?" and they said she had gone away. Well, home had lost its charm to me; it was that mother who made home so sweet to everyone; it is the presence of the loved ones that will make heaven so sweet to all of us. Christ is there; God, the Father, is there; and many, many who were dear to us when they lived on earth are there—and we shall be with them by and by.

We find clearly in the eighteenth chapter of Matthew, tenth verse, that the angels are there: "Take heed that ye despise not one of these little ones; for I say unto you, That in heaven their angels do always behold the face of my Father which is in heaven."

"Their angels do always behold the Father's face!" We shall have good company up there; not only those who have been redeemed, but those angels who have never been lost; who have never known what it is to transgress; who have never known what it is to be disobedient; who have obeyed Him from the very morning of creation.

It says in Luke 1, when Gabriel came down to

tell Zacharias that he was to be the father of the forerunner of Jesus Christ, Zacharias doubted him; he had never been doubted before; and that doubt is met with the declaration: "I am Gabriel, that stand in the presence of God" (v. 19) What a glorious thing to be able to say!

It has been said that there will be three things which will surprise us when we get to heaven— one, to find many whom we did not expect to find there; another, to find some not there whom we had expected; a third, and perhaps the greatest wonder—to find ourselves there.

A poor woman once told Rowland Hill that the way to heaven was short, easy, and simple; comprising only three steps—out of self, into Christ, and into glory. We have a shorter way now—out of self and into Christ, and we are there. As a dead man cannot inherit an estate, no more can a dead soul inherit heaven. The soul must be raised up in Christ.

Among the good whom we hope to meet in heaven, we are told, there will be every variety of character, taste, and disposition. There is not one mansion there; there are many. The gates of heaven are twelve in number. There are not only three gates on the north, but on the east three gates, and on the west three gates, and on the south three gates. From opposite standpoints of the Christian world, from different quarters of human life and character, through various expressions of their common faith and hope, through diverse modes of conversion, through different portions of the Holy Scripture will the weary travelers enter the Heavenly City, and meet each other—"not without surprise"—on the shores of the same river of life.

And on those shores they will find a tree bearing, not the same kind of fruit always and at all times, but "twelve manner of fruits," for every different turn of mind—for the patient sufferer, for the active servant, for the holy and humble philosopher, for the spirits of just men now at last made perfect; and "the leaves of the tree" shall be "for the healing," not of one single church or people only, but "of the nations"—the Frenchman, the German, the Italian, the Russian—for all those from whom it may be, in this world, its fruits have been farthest removed, but who, nevertheless, have "hungered and thirsted after righteousness" and who therefore "shall be filled" (Revelation 22:2; Matthew 5:6).

An eminent preacher says: "When I was a boy, I thought of heaven as a great, shining city, with vast walls and domes and spires, and with nobody in it except white-robed angels, who were strangers to me. By and by my little brother died; and I thought of a great city with walls and domes and spires, and a flock of cold, unknown angels, and one little fellow that I was acquainted with. He was the only one that I knew at that time. Then another brother died; and there were two that I knew. Then my acquaintances began to die; and the flock continually grew. But it was not until I had sent one of my little children to his Heavenly Parent—God—that I began to think I had a little in myself. A second went, a third went, a fourth went; and by that time I had so many acquaintances in heaven, that I did not see any more walls and domes and spires. I began to think of the residents of the celestial city as my friends. And now so many of my acquaintances have gone there, that it sometimes seems to me that I know more people in Heaven than I do on earth."

We Shall Live Forever

It says in John 12:26, "If any man serve me, let him follow me; and where I am, there shall also my servant be."

I cannot agree with some people that Paul has been sleeping in the grave and is still there after the storms of many hundred years. I cannot believe that he who loved the Master, who had such a burning zeal for Him, has been separated from Him in an unconscious state. "Father, I will that they also, whom thou hast given me, be with me where I am; that they may behold my glory, which thou hast given me" (John 17:24). This is Christ's prayer.

Now when a man believes on the Lord Jesus Christ, he receives eternal life. A great many people make a mistake right there; "He that believeth on the Son hath—h-a-t-h—hath eternal life"; it does not say he shall have it when he comes to die; it is in the present tense; it is mine now—if I believe. It is the gift of God, that is enough. You can not bury eternal life. All the grave diggers in the world cannot dig a grave large enough and deep enough to hold eternal life; all the coffin-makers in the world cannot make a coffin large enough and strong enough to hold eternal life; it is mine; it is mine!

I believe when Paul said, "To be absent from the body" is "to be present with the Lord" (2 Corinthians 5:8), he meant what he said: that he was not going to be separated from Him for many hundred years; the spirit that was given him when he was converted he had from a new life and a new nature, and they could not lay that away in the sepulchre; they could not bury it. That flew to meet its Maker. Even the body shall be raised; this body, sown in dishonor, shall be raised in glory; this body which has known corruption, shall put on incorruption, and this mortal shall put on immortality. It is only a question of time. The great morning of the world will, by and by, dawn upon the earth, and the dead shall come forth and shall hear the voice of Him who is "the resurrection and the life."

Paul says: "If our earthly house of this tabernacle were dissolved, we have a building of God, a house not made with hands, eternal in the heavens" (2 Corinthians 5:1). He could take down the clay temple, and leave that, but he had a better house. He says in the first chapter of Philippians: "I am in a strait betwixt two, having a desire to depart, and be with Christ; which is far better; nevertheless to abide in the flesh is more needful for you" (v. 23–24). To me, it is a sweet thought to think that death does not separate us from the Master. A great many people are living continually in the bondage of death, but if I have eternal life, death cannot touch that; it may touch the house I live in; it may change my countenance and send my body away to the grave, but it cannot touch this new life.

To me it is very sad to think that so many professed Christians look upon death as they do. I personally received a letter from a friend in London, and I thought, as I read it, I would take it and show it to other people and see if I could not get them to look upon death as this friend does. He had lost his beloved mother. In England it is a very common thing to send out cards in memory of the departed ones, and they put upon them great borders of black—sometimes a quarter of an inch of black border—but this friend had put on a gold border; he did not put on black at all; his mother had gone to the golden city, and so he put on a golden border; and I think it a good deal better than black. I think when our friends die, instead of putting a great black border upon our memorials to make them look dark, it would be better for us to put on gold.

It is not death at all; it is life. Someone said to a person dying: "Well, you are in the land of the living yet." "No," said he, "I am in the land of the dying yet, but I am going to the land of the living; they live there and never die." This is the land of sin and death and tears, but up yonder they never die. It is perpetual life; it is unceasing joy.

"It is a glorious thing to die," was the testimony of Hannah Moore on her deathbed, though her life had been sown thick with the rarest friendships and age had not so weakened her memory as to cause her to forget those little hamlets among the cliffs of her native hills, or the mission schools she had with such perseverance established and where she would be so sadly missed.

As James Montgomery has said:

> There is a soft, a downy bed;
> 'Tis fair as breath of even;
> A couch for weary mortals spread,

Where they may rest the aching head,
    And find repose—in heaven!

There is an hour of peaceful rest,
    To mourning wanderers given.
There is a joy for souls distressed,
A balm for every wounded breast,
    'Tis found alone—in heaven!

Knowing Our Friends

Many are anxious to know if they will recognize their friends in heaven. In the eighth chapter of Matthew and the eleventh verse, we read: "And I say unto you, That many shall come from the east and west, and shall sit down with Abraham, and Isaac, and Jacob, in the kingdom of heaven."

Here we find that Abraham, who lived so many hundreds of years before Christ, had not lost his identity, and Christ tells us that the time is coming when they shall come from the east and west and shall sit down with Abraham and Isaac and Jacob in the kingdom of God. These men had not lost their identity; they were known as Abraham, Isaac, and Jacob. And if you will turn to that wonderful scene that took place on the Mount of Transfiguration, you will find that Moses, who had been gone from the earth fifteen hundred years, was there; Peter, James, and John saw him on the Mount of Transfiguration; they saw him as Moses; he had not lost his name. Christ says of him that overcometh, "I will not blot his name out of the [Lamb's] book of life" (Revelation 3:5). We have names in heaven; we are going to bear our names there; we will be known.

Over in the Psalms it says: "I shall be satisfied, when I awake, with thy likeness" (17:15). That is enough. *Want* is written on every human heart down here, but there we shall be satisfied. You may hunt the world from one end to the other, and you will not find a man or woman who is satisfied; but in heaven we shall want for nothing. In the third chapter of the first epistle of John, we read these words addressed to followers of Christ:

> Beloved, now are we the sons of God, and it doth not yet appear what we shall be: but we know that when he shall appear, we shall be like him; for we shall see him as he is. And every man that hath this hope in him purifieth himself, even as he is pure. (vv. 2–3)

Moreover, it seems highly probable, indeed I think it is clearly taught by Scripture, that a great many careless Christians will get into heaven. There will be a great many who will get in "by the skin of their teeth," or as Lot was saved from Sodom, "so as by fire" (see 1 Corinthians 3:15). They will barely get in, but there will be no crown of rejoicing. But *everybody* is not going to rush into heaven. There are a great many who will *not* be there. You know we have a class of people who tell us they are going into the kingdom of God whether they are converted or not. They tell us that they are on their way, that they are going there. They tell us all are going there; that the good, the bad, and indifferent are all going into the kingdom, and that they will all be there; that there is no difference; and, in other words—if I may be allowed to use plain language—they give God the lie.

But they say, "We believe in the *mercy* of God"; so do I. I believe in the *justice* of God too; and I think heaven would be a good deal worse than this earth if unrenewed men were permitted to form part of it.

Why, if a man should live forever in this world in sin, what would become of this world? It seems as if it would be *hell itself*. Let your mind pass over the history of this country and think of some who have lived in it. Suppose they should never die; suppose they should live on and on forever in sin and rebellion. Do you think that God is going to take those men who have rejected his Son, who have spurned the offer of His mercy, who have refused salvation and have trampled against His laws down here? Do you suppose God is going to take them right into His Kingdom and let them live there forever? By no means.

No Drunkards in Heaven

"Be not deceived . . . nor thieves, nor covetous, nor *drunkards*, nor revilers, nor extortioners, shall inherit the kingdom of God" (1 Corinthians 6:9–10).

"No drunkard shall inherit the kingdom of God." Now let those mothers who have sons who are just commencing a dissipated life wake up; and rest not day nor night until their boys are converted by the power of God's grace, because *no drunkard shall inherit the kingdom of God*. Many of these moderate drinkers will become drunkards; no man ever became a drunkard all at once. How the devil blinds these moderate drinkers! I do not know of any sin more binding than the sin of intemperance; the man is bound hand and foot before he knows it.

I was reading some time ago an account of snake worshiping in India. I thought it was a horrible thing. I read of a mother who saw a snake come into her home and coil itself around her little infant only six months old, and she thought the reptile was such a sacred thing that she did not dare to touch it; and she saw the snake destroy her child; she heard the child's pitiful cries but dared not rescue it. My soul revolted as I read the narrative. But I do not know but we have things right here in America that are just as bad as that serpent in India —serpents that are coming into many a Christian home and coiling around many a son and binding them hand and foot, and the fathers and mothers seem to be asleep.

Oh, may the Spirit of God wake us up! No drunkard shall inherit the kingdom of God; nor rum seller either. Bear that in mind. "Woe unto him that giveth his neighbour drink, that putteth thy bottle to him" (Habakkuk 2:15). I pity any professing Christians who rent their property for drinking taverns; I pity them from the depths of my heart. If you ever expect to inherit the kingdom of God, give it up. If you can never rent your property to better purposes you had better let it stand empty. This idea that all is going well, and that all are going to the kingdom of God, whether they repent or not, is not taught anywhere in the Scripture.

There will be no extortioners in heaven, those men who are taking advantage of their brothers and those who have been unfortunate, whose families are sick, who have had to mortgage their property and had snap-judgment taken against them by some man who has his hand at their throat and takes every cent that he can get. That man is an extortioner. He shall not inherit the kingdom of God. I pity a man who gets money dishonestly. See the trouble he has to keep it. It is sure to be scattered. If you got it dishonestly you cannot keep it; your children can't keep it—they have not the power. You see that all over the country. A man who gets a dollar dishonestly had better make restitution and pay it back very quickly, or it will burn in his pocket.

Some Will Not Get In

In the days of Noah we read that he sailed over the deluge. He was the only righteous man, but according to the theory of some people, the rest of those men who were so foul and so wicked—too wicked to live—God took them and swept them all into heaven, and left the only righteous man to go through this trial. Drunkards and thieves and vagabonds all went to heaven, they say. You might as well go forward and preach that "you can swear as much as you like, and murder as much as you please, and it will come out right—that God will forgive you; God is so merciful."

Suppose the governor of a state should pardon every person that the courts ever convicted and are now lying in its jails and penitentiaries; suppose he should let them all loose because he is so merciful that he could not bear to have men punished; I think he would not be governor of that state long. These men who are talking about God being so full of mercy, that He is going to spare and take all men to heaven, would be the very men to say that such a governor as that ought to be impeached

—that he ought not to be governor. Let us bear in mind that the Scripture says there is a certain class of people who *"shall not inherit the kingdom of God."* Now, I will give you the Scripture; it is a good deal better to just give the Scripture for these things, and then if you do not like it you can quarrel with Scripture and not with me. Let no man say that I have been saying who is going to heaven and who is not; I will let the Scripture speak for itself: "Know ye not that the unrighteous shall not inherit the kingdom of God?" (1 Corinthians 6:9).

But the unrighteous—the adulterers, the fornicators and thieves—these men may all inherit it if they will only turn away from their sins. "Let the wicked forsake his way, and the unrighteous man his thoughts" (Isaiah 55:7); but if the unrighteous man says, "I will not turn away from sin; I will hold on to sin and have heaven," he is deceiving himself.

A man who steals my pocketbook loses a good deal more than I do. I can afford to let him have my pocketbook a great deal better than he can afford to take it. See how much that man who steals my pocketbook loses. Perhaps he may get a few dollars; or he may steal my coat; but he does not get much. See how much he has lost. Take an inventory of what the man loses if he loses heaven. Think of it. No thief shall inherit the kingdom of God. To any thief I would say: "Steal no more." Let him ask God to forgive him; let him repent of his sin and turn to God. If you get eternal life it is worth more than the whole world. If you were to steal the whole world, you would not get much, after all. The whole world does not amount to much if you have not eternal life with it to enjoy yourself in the future.

THE WHITE-ROBED SAINTS

Who are they whose songs are sounding
    O'er the golden harps above?
Hark! they tell of grace abounding,
    And Jehovah's sovereign love.

Who are they that keep their station
    Round the great eternal throne?
They from earthly tribulation
    To their heavenly rest are gone.

See their robes of dazzling whiteness,
    Without blemish, spot, or stain;
See their crowns that grow in brightness,
    Purchased by the Lamb once slain.

Never heat shall beat upon them,
    Thirst nor hunger reach them there;
He, whose life from death hath won them,
    Bids them now His glory share.

Feeble hearts are nerved for duty,
    Faltering feet now firmly stand.
Palms of heaven's unfading beauty
    Mark earth's once despiséd band.

'Tis the Lamb of God who leads them,
    And they serve Him night and day;
By the heavenly fount He feeds them,
    He hath wiped their tears away.

Sweet their theme! 'Tis still, "Salvation
    Unto Christ, the Holy One!"
And their sighs of tribulation
    Change to songs around the throne.

                    Anna Shipton

HEAVEN
Its Happiness

"WHAT! ALMOST HOME?"

"What! Almost home?" "Yes, almost home," she said,
And light seemed gleaming on her aged head.
"Jesus is very precious!" Those who near
Her bedside stood were thrilled those words to hear.
"Toward His blest home I turn my willing feet;
Hinder me not; I go my Lord to meet."
Silence ensued. She seemed to pass away,
Serene and quiet as that summer day.
"Speak," cried through tears her daughter, bending low,
"One word, beloved mother, ere you go."
She spoke that word; the last she spoke on earth,
In whispering tones—that word of wondrous worth:
"JESUS!" The sorrowing listeners caught the sound,
But angels heard it with a joy profound.
Back, at its mighty power, the gates unfold—
The gates of pearl that guard the streets of gold.
The harpers with their harps took up the strain,
And sang the triumph of the Lord again,
As through the open portals entered in
Another soul redeemed from death and sin.
And as from earth the spirit passed away,
To dwell forever in the realms of day,
Those who were left to mourn could almost hear
The strains of heavenly music strike the ear.
And to their longing eyes by grace was given,
In such a scene, as 'twere, a glimpse of heaven.

—Unknown

3

Its Happiness

Eye hath not seen, nor ear heard, neither hath it entered into the heart of man, the things which God hath prepared for them that love him.
1 Corinthians 2:9; see Isaiah 64:4

If there is one word above another that will swing open the eternal gates, it is the name of Jesus. There are a great many passwords and bywords down here, but that will be the countersign up above. Jesus Christ is the "Open Sesame" to heaven. Anyone who tries to climb up some other way is a thief and a robber. But when we get in, what a joy above every other joy we can think of will it be to see Jesus Himself all the time and to be with him continually.

Isaiah has given this promise of God to everyone who is saved through faith: "Thine eyes shall see the king in his beauty; they shall behold the land that is very far off" (33:17). Some of us may not be able to go around the world. We may not be able to see any of the foreign countries; but every Christian by and by is going to see a land that is very far off. This is our Promised Land. John Milton says of the saints who have gone already:

They walk with God
High in Salvation, and the climes of bliss.

It is blissful climate up there. People down here look around a great deal to find a good climate where they will not be troubled by any of their pains or aches, but the climate of heaven is so fine that no pains or aches can hold out against it. There will be no room to find fault. We shall leave all our pains and aches behind us and find an everlasting health, such as earth can never know.

But you know the glory of Christ as reigning King of heaven would be something too much for *mortal* eyes to endure. In the sixth chapter of 1 Timothy, we read of Christ as

the blessed and only Potentate, the King of kings, and Lord of lords; who only hath immortality, dwelling in the light which no man can approach unto; whom no man hath seen, nor can see. (vv. 15–16)

As mortals, we cannot see that light. Our feeble faculties would be dazzled before such a blaze of glory.

In Ezekiel 1:28, we read of that prophet having a faint glimpse of it:

As the appearance of the bow that is in the cloud in the day of rain, so was the appearance of the brightness round about. This was the appearance of the likeness of the glory of the Lord. And when I saw it, I fell upon my face.

We are amazed at ordinary perfections now. None of us can look the sun squarely in the face. But when this corruptible shall have put on incorruption, as Paul says, the power of the soul will be stronger. We shall be able to see Christ in His glory then. Though the moon be confounded and the sun ashamed, yet we shall see Him as He is. This is what will make heaven so happy.

We all know that great happiness cannot be found on earth. Reason, revelation, and the experience of six thousand years all tell us that. No human creature has the power to give it. Even doing good fails to give it fully, for, owing to sin in the world, even the best have not perfect happiness here. They have to wait for heaven, although they may be so near it sometimes that they can see heralds of its joy and beauty, as Columbus saw the strange and beautiful birds hovering around his ships long before he caught sight of America.

All the joys we are to know in heaven will come from the presence of God. This is the leading thought in all that the Scripture has to say on the subject. What life on this earth is without health, life in heaven would be without the presence of God. God's presence will be the very light and life of the place. It is said that one translation of the words describing the presence of God is "a happy-making sight." It will be a sight like the return of a long-lost boy to his mother, or the first glimpse of your home after you have been a long time away. Some of you know how a little sunshine on a dark day, or the face of a kind friend in trouble, often cheers us up. Well, it will be something like that, only a thousand times better. Our perceptions of

God will be clearer then, and that will make us love Him all the more.

The more we know God, the more we love Him. A great many of us would love God more if we only became better acquainted with him. While on earth it gives Christians great pleasure to think of the perfection of Jesus Christ, but how will it be when we see Him as He is?

We Shall Be Like Christ

Someone once asked a Christian what he expected to do when he got to heaven. He said he expected to spend the first thousand years looking at Jesus Christ, and after that he would look for Peter, and then for James, and for John; and all the time he could conceive of would be joyfully filled with looking upon these great persons. But it seems to me that one look at Jesus Christ will more than reward us for all we have ever done for Him down here, for all the sacrifices we can possibly make for Him, just to see Him; only to see Him. But we shall become like Him when we once have seen Him, because we shall have His Spirit. Jesus, the Savior of the world, will be there, and we shall see Him face-to-face.

It will not be the pearly gates, nor the jasper walls, nor the streets paved with transparent gold that will make it heaven to us. These would not satisfy us. If these were all, we would not want to stay there forever. I heard of a child whose mother was very sick; and while she lay very low, one of the neighbors took the child away to stay with her until the mother should be well again. But instead of getting better, the mother died; and they thought

they would not take the child home until the funeral was all over; and would never tell her about
her mother being dead. So a while afterward they
brought the little girl home.

First she went into the sitting room to find her
mother; then she went into the parlor to find her
mother there; and she went from one end of the
house to the other and could not find her. At last
she said, "Where is my mama?" And when they
told her her mama was gone, the little thing wanted to go back to the neighbor's house again. Home
had lost its attraction to her since her mother was
not there any longer. No, it will not be the jasper
walls and the pearly gates that will make heaven
attractive. It is our being with God. We shall be in
the presence of the Redeemer; we shall be forever
with the Lord.

There was a time when I used to think more of
Jesus Christ than I did of the Father; Christ
seemed to be so much nearer to me because he had
become the arbiter between me and God. In my
imagination I put God away on the throne as a
stern judge, but Christ had come in as the Media-
tor, and it seemed as if Christ was much nearer to
me than God the Father. I got over that years ago,
when God gave me a son, and for ten years I had
an only son, and as I looked at the child as he grew
up, the thought came to me that it took more love
for God to give up His Son than it did for His Son
to die. Think of the love that God had for this
world when He gave Christ up!

If you will turn to Acts 7:55, you will find that
when Stephen was being stoned he lifted up his
eyes, and it seemed as if God rolled back the cur-

tain of time and allowed him to look into the eternal city and see Christ standing at the right hand of God. When Jesus Christ went on high He led captivity captive and took His seat, for His work was done; but when Stephen saw Him he was standing up, and I can imagine He saw that martyr fighting, as it were, single-handed and alone, the first martyr, though many were to come after him. You can hear the tramp of the millions coming after him to lay down their lives for the Son of God. But Stephen led the van; he was the first martyr. And as he was dying for the Lord Jesus Christ he looked up. Christ was standing to give him a welcome, and the Holy Ghost came down to bear witness that Christ was there. How then can we doubt it?

A beggar does not enjoy looking at a palace. The grandeur of its architecture is lost upon him. Looking upon a royal banquet does not satisfy the hunger of a starving man. *But seeing heaven is also having a share in it.* There would be no joy there if we did not feel that some of it was ours. God unites the soul to Himself. We read in 2 Peter that we are made "partakers of the divine nature" (1:4). Now if you put a piece of iron in the fire, it very soon loses its dark color and becomes red and hot like the fire, but it does not lose its iron nature. So the soul becomes bright with God's brightness, beautiful with God's beauty, pure with God's purity, and warm with the glow of His perfect love, and yet remains a human soul. We shall be like Him, but remain ourselves.

There is a fable that a kindhearted king was once hunting in a forest and found a blind orphan boy, who was living almost like a beast. The king was touched with pity and adopted the boy as his own and had him taught all that can be learned by one who is blind. When he reached his twenty-first year, the king, who was also a great physician, restored the youth his sight and took him to his palace, where surrounded by his nobles and all the majesty and magnificence of his court, he proclaimed him one of his sons and commanded all to give him their honor and love. The once friendless orphan thus became a prince and a sharer in the royal dignity and of all the happiness and glory to be found in the palace of a king. Who can tell the joy that overwhelmed the soul of that young man when he first saw the king, of whose beauty and goodness and power he had heard so much? Who can tell the happiness he must have felt when he saw his own princely attire and found himself adopted into the royal family—honored and beloved by all?

Now Christ is the great and mighty King who finds our souls in the wilderness of this sinful world. He finds us, as we read in the third chapter of Revelation, "wretched, and miserable, and poor, and blind, and naked" (v. 17). We read in the first chapter of the same book that He "washed us from our sins in his own blood" (v. 5); and again, in the sixty-first chapter of Isaiah, He has clothed us with a spotless robe of innocence, "with the garments of salvation"; He has covered us "with a robe of righteousness, as a bridegroom decketh himself with ornaments, and as a bride adorneth herself with her jewels" (v. 10).

The mission of the Gospel to sinners, as we find it in the twenty-sixth chapter of Acts, was "to open their eyes, and to turn them from darkness to light, and from the power of Satan unto God, that they may receive forgiveness of sins, and inheritance among them which are sanctified by faith that is in me" (v. 18). This is what Christ has done for every Christian. He has adorned you with the gift of grace and adopted you as His child; and as it says in the third chapter of 1 Corinthians:

> All things are yours; whether Paul, or Apollos, or Cephas, or the world, or life, or death, or things present, or things to come; all are yours; and ye are Christ's; and Christ is God's. (vv. 21–22)

He has given you His own Word to educate you for heaven; He has opened your eyes so that now you see. By His grace and your own cooperation your soul is being gradually developed into a more perfect resemblance to Him.

Finally, your heavenly Father calls you home, where you will see the angels and saints clothed with the beauty of Christ Himself, standing around His throne and hearing the word that will admit you into their society: "Well done, thou good and faithful servant: . . . enter thou into the joy of thy Lord" (Matthew 25:21). In the sixteenth chapter of John, Christ Himself says: "All things that the Father hath are mine: therefore . . . he shall take of mine, and shall shew it unto you" (v. 15). All will be yours. Ah, how poor and mean do earthly pleasures seem by comparison! How true those lines of a Scots poet:

The world can never give
The bliss for which we sigh;
'Tis not the whole of life to live,
Nor all of death to die.
Beyond this vale of tears
There is a life above,
Unmeasured by the flight of years,
And all that life is love.

Over the River

There is joy in heaven, we are told, over the conversions that take place on earth. In Luke 15:7, we read: "I say unto you, that likewise joy shall be in heaven over one sinner that repenteth, more than over ninety and nine just persons, which need no repentance." When there is going to be an election for president of the United States there is tremendous excitement—a great commotion. There is probably not a paper from Maine to California that would not have something on nearly every page about the candidates; the whole country is excited; but I doubt if it would be noticed in heaven. If a monarch should leave his throne, there would be great excitement throughout the nations of the earth; the whole world would be interested in the event; it would be telegraphed around the world; but it would be probably be overlooked altogether in heaven. Yet if one little boy or girl, one man or woman, would repent of his sins, this day and hour that would be noticed in heaven.

They look at things differently up there. Things that look very large to us look very small in heaven; and things that seem very small to us down here may be very great up yonder. Think of it! By an act of our own, we may cause joy in heaven. The thought seems almost too wonderful to understand. To think that the poorest sinner on earth, by an act of his own, can send a thrill of joy through the hosts of heaven!

The Bible says: "There is joy in the presence of the angels" (Luke 15:10); not that the angels rejoice, but it is "in the presence" of the angels. I have studied over that a great deal and often wondered what it meant. "Joy in the presence of the angels"? Now it is speculation; I admit it may be true, or it may not; but perhaps the friends who have left the shores of time—they who have gone within the fold—may be looking down upon us; and when they see one they prayed for while on earth repenting and turning to God, it sends a thrill of joy to their very hearts. Even now, some mother who has gone up yonder may be looking down upon a son or daughter, and if that child should say: "I will meet that mother of mine; I will repent; yes, I am going to join you, Mother," the news, with the speed of a sunbeam, reaches heaven, and that mother may then rejoice, as we read, "in the presence of the angels."

In Dublin, after one of the meetings, a man walked into the inquiry room with his daughter, his only one, whose mother had died some time before, and he prayed: "O God, let this truth go deep into my daughter's heart, and grant that the prayers of her mother may be answered today— that she may be saved." As they rose up she put her arms about his neck and kissed him and said: "I want to meet my mother; I want to be a Christian." That day she accepted Christ. That man was a minister in Texas. The daughter died out there a little while ago, and is now with her mother in heaven. What a blessed and joyful meeting it must have been! It may be a sister, it may be a brother, who is beckoning you over:

Over the river they beckon to me,
    Loved ones who've crossed to the farther side;
The gleam of their snowy robes I see,
    But their voices are drowned in the rushing tide.
There's one with ringlets of sunny gold,
    And eyes, the reflection of heaven's own blue;
He crossed in the twilight gray and cold,
    And the pale mist hid him from mortal view.
We saw not the angels who met him there,
    The gates of the city we could not see;
Over the river, over the river,
    My brother stands waiting to welcome me.

Whoever you are, do not delay.

The story is told of a father who had his little daughter out late in the evening. The night was dark, and they had passed through a thick wood to the brink of a river. Far away on the opposite shore a light twinkled here and there in the few scattered houses, and still farther off blazed the bright lights of the great city to which they were going. The little child was weary and sleepy, and the father held her in his arms while he waited for the ferryman, who was at the other side. At length they saw a little light; nearer and nearer came the sound of the oars, and soon they were safe in the boat.

"Father," said the little girl.

"Well, my child?"

"It's very dark, and I can't see the shore: where are we going?"

"The ferryman knows the way, little one; we will soon be over."

"Oh, I wish we were there, Father."

Soon in her home loving arms welcomed her, and her fears and her tremor were gone. Some months pass by, and this little child stands on the brink of a river that is darker and deeper, more terrible still. It is the River of Death. The same loving father stands near her, distressed that his child must cross this river and he not be able to go with her. For days and for nights he and her mother have been watching over her, leaving her bedside only long enough for their meals, and to pray for the life of their precious one. For hours she has been slumbering, and it seems as if her spirit must pass away without her waking again, but just before the morning watch she suddenly awakes with the eye bright, the reason unclouded, and every faculty alive. A sweet smile is playing upon her face.

"Father," she says, "I have come again to the riverside, and am again waiting for the ferryman to come and take me across."

"Does it seem as dark and cold as when you went over the other river, my child?"

"Oh, no! There is no darkness here. The river is covered with floating silver. The boat coming toward me seems made of solid light, and I am not afraid of the ferryman."

"Can you see over the river, my darling?"

"Oh, yes, there is a great and beautiful city there, all filled with light; and I hear music such as the angels make!"

"Do you see anyone on the other side?"

"Why yes, yes, I see the most beautiful form; and He beckons me now to come. Oh, ferryman, make haste! I know who it is! It is Jesus; my own blessed Jesus. I shall be caught in His arms. I shall rest on His bosom—I come—I COME."

And thus she crossed over the River of Death, made like a silver stream by the presence of the blessed Redeemer.

Something More

There is hardly an unconverted man any where, no matter how high up or how rich he may be, but will tell you, if you get his confidence, that he is not happy. There is something he wants that he cannot get, or there is something he has that he wants to get rid of. It is very doubtful if the ruler of Russia is a happy man, and yet he has about all he can get. Although the English queen has palaces and millions at her command, and has besides what most sovereigns lack, the love of her subjects, it is a question whether she gets great pleasure out of her position. If kings and queens love Jesus Christ and are saved, then they may be happy. If they know they will reach heaven like the humblest of their subjects, then they may rest secure. Paul, the humble tent-maker, will have a higher seat in heaven than the best and greatest sovereign that ever ruled the earth. If a ruler should meet John Bunyan, the poor tinker, up in heaven, he no doubt would find him the greater man.

The Christian life is the only happy one. Without it something is always wanting. When we are young we have grand enterprises, but we soon spoil them by being too rash. We want experience. When we get old we have the experience, but then all the power to carry out our schemes is gone. "Happy is that people, whose God is the Lord" (Psalm 144:15).

The only way to be happy is to be good. The man who steals from necessity sins because he is afraid of being unhappy, but for the moment he forgets all about how unhappy the sin is going to make him. Bad as he is, man is the best and noblest thing on earth, and it is easy to understand how he fails to find true happiness in anything lower than himself. The only object better than ourselves is God, and He is all we can ever be satisfied with. Gold, which is mere dross dug up out of the earth, does not satisfy man. Neither do the honor and praise of other men. The human soul wants something more than that. Heaven is the only place to get it. No wonder that the angels who see God all the time are so happy.

The publicans went to hunt up John the Baptist in the wilderness, to know what they should do. Some of the the highest men in the land went to consult the hermit to know how to get happiness. "Whosoever trusteth in the Lord, happy is he" (Proverbs 16:20). It is because there is *no* real happiness down here, that earth is not worth living for. It is because it is *all* above, that heaven is worth dying for. In heaven there is all life and no death. In hell there is all death and no life. Here on earth there are both living and dying, which is between the two. If we are dead to sin here we will live in heaven, and if we live in sin here we must expect eternal death to follow.

Do you know that every Christian dies twice? He first becomes spiritually dead to sin—that is the renewed soul. He then begins to feel the joy of heaven. The joys of heaven reach down to earth as many and as sure as the rays of the sun. Then comes physical death, which makes way for the physical heaven. Of course the old sinful body has to be changed. We cannot take that into heaven. It will be a glorified body that we will get at the resurrection, not a sinful body. Our bodies will be transfigured like Christ's.

There will be no temptation in heaven. If there were no temptation in the world now, God could not prove us. He wants to see if we are loyal. That is why He put the forbidden tree in Paradise; that accounts for the presence of the Canaanite in the land of Israel. When we plant a seed, after a time it disappears and brings forth a seed that looks much the same, but still it is a different seed. So our bodies and the bodies of those we know and love will be raised up, looking much the same—but still not all the same.

Christ took the same body into heaven that was crucified on the cross, unless He was transformed in the cloud after the disciples lost sight of Him. There must have been some change in the appearance of Christ after His resurrection, for Mary Magdalene, who was the first one who saw Him, did not know Him; neither did the disciples, who walked and talked with Him about Himself, and did not recognize Him until He began to ask a blessing at supper. Even Peter did not know Him when He appeared on the seashore. Thomas would not believe it was Christ until he saw the prints of the nails and the wound in His side. But we shall all know Him in heaven.

There are two things that the Bible makes as clear and certain as eternity. One is that we are going to see Christ, and the other that we are going to be like Him. God will never hide His face from us there, and Satan will never show his.

There is not such a great difference between grace and glory after all. Grace is the bud, and glory the blossom. Grace is glory begun, and glory is grace perfected. It will not come hard to people who are serving God down here to do it when they go up yonder. They will change places, but they will not change employments.

Higher Up

The moment a person becomes heavenly minded and gets his heart and affections set on things above, then life becomes beautiful, the light of heaven shines across his pathway, and he does not have to be all the time lashing and upbraiding himself because he is not more like Christ. Someone asked a Scotsman if he was on the way to heaven, and he said: "Why man, I live there; I am not on the way." That is just it. We want to *live* in heaven; while we are walking in this world it is our privilege to have our hearts and affections there.

I once heard Mr. Morehouse tell a story about a lady in London who found one of those poor, bedridden saints, and then she found a wealthy woman who was all the time complaining and murmuring at her lot. Sometimes I think people whom God does the most for in worldly things think the less of Him and care less about Him and are the most unproductive in His service. But this lady went around as a missionary visiting the poor, and she used to go and visit the poor, bedridden saint, and she said if she wanted to get cheered up and her heart made happy she would go and visit her.

[There is a place in Chicago, and has been for years, where a great many Christians have always gone when they want to get their faith strengthened; they go there and visit one of these saints. And a friend told me that she thought that the Lord kept one of those saints in most of the cities to entertain angels as they passed over the cities on errands of mercy, for it seems that these saints are often visited by the heavenly host.] Well, this lady missionary had wanted to get this wealthy woman in contact with this saint, and she invited her to go a number of times; finally the lady consented to go. And when she got to the place, she went up the first flight of stairs, and it was not very clean and was dark.

"What a horrible place," the lady said; "why did you bring me here?"

The lady smiled and said: "It is better higher up."

And then they went up another flight, and it didn't grow any lighter and she complained again and the lady said, "It is better higher up." And then they went up another flight, and it was no lighter; still the missionary kept saying, "It is better higher up." And when they got to the fifth story they opened the door and entered a beautiful room, a room that was carpeted, with plants in the window. A little bird was in a cage singing, and there was that saint just smiling. And the first thing the complaining woman had to say to her was, "It must be very hard for you to be here and suffer."

"Oh, that is a very small thing; it is not very hard," she said, "it is better higher up."

And so if things do not go just right, if they do not go to suit us here, we can say, "It is better higher up, it is better farther on," and we can lift up our hearts and rejoice as we journey on toward HOME.

You know those beautiful lines:

> Beyond the smiling and the weeping,
>   I shall be soon;
> Beyond the waking and the sleeping,
> Beyond the sowing and the reaping,
>   I shall be soon.
> Love, rest, and home!
>   Sweet Home!
> Lord, tarry not, but come.
> Beyond the rising and the setting,
>   I shall be soon;
> Beyond the calming and the fretting,
> Beyond remembering and forgetting,
>   I shall be soon.
> Love, rest, and home!
>   Sweet Hope!
> Lord, tarry not, but come.

SPIRIT VOICES

Nearer and nearer, day by day, the distant voices
    come;
Soft through the pearly gate they swell, and seem to
    call me home.
The lamp of life burns faint and low; aye, let it fainter
    burn;
For who would weep the failing lamp when birds an-
    nounce the morn?
I saw the faces of my loved gleam through the twi-
    light dim,
And softly on the morning air arose the heaven-born
    hymn;
With looks of love they gazed on me, as none gaze on
    me now;
The glory of the Infinite surrounded every brow.
Fair lilies, star-like in their bloom, and waving palms
    they bore,
And oh, the smiles of peace and joy those heavenly
    faces wore!
Thou who hast fathomed death's dark tide, save me
    from death's alarms;
Beneath my trembling soul, oh, stretch Thine ever-
    lasting arms!
No second cross, no thorny crown can bruise Thy sa-
    cred brow;
Thou who the wine-press trod alone, o'er the dark
    waves bear me now.
A parting hour, a pang of pain, and then shall pass
    away
The veil that shrouds Thee where Thou reign'st in
    everlasting day.

No sin, no sigh, no withering fear, can wring the bosom there;
But basking in Thy smile I shall Thy sinless service share.
How long, Oh Lord, how long before Thou'lt take me by the hand,
And I, Thy weakest child, at least among Thy children stand?
Beyond the stars that steadfast shine my spirit pines to soar,
To dwell within my Father's house, and leave that home no more.
O Lord, Thou hast with angel food my fainting spirit fed;
If 'tis Thy will I linger here, bless Thou the path I tread;
And though my soul doth pant to pass within the pearly gate,
Yet teach me for thy summons, Lord, in patience still to wait.

Anna Shipton

HEAVEN
Its Certainty

I SHINE IN THE LIGHT OF GOD

I shine in the light of God;
  His likeness stamps my brow;
Through the Valley of Death my feet have trod,
  And I reign in glory now!

No breaking heart is here,
  No keen and thrilling pain,
No wasted cheek where the frequent tear
  Hath rolled and left its stain.

* * *

O friends of mortal years,
  The trusted and the true,
Ye are watching still in the valley of tears,
  But I wait to welcome you.

Do I forget? O no!
  For memory's golden chain
Shall bind *my* heart to the hearts below
  Till they meet to touch again.

Each link is strong and bright,
  And love's electric flame
Flows freely down, like a river of light,
  To the world from whence I came.

Do you mourn when another star
  Shines out from the glittering sky?
Do you weep when the raging voice of war
  And the storms of conflict die?

Then why should your tears run down,
  And your hearts be sorely riven,
For another gem in the Savior's crown,
  And another soul in heaven?
                    —From an English Friend

4
Its Certainty

*In My Father's house are many mansions. . . . I
go to prepare a place for you.*　　　John 14:2

There are some people who depend so much
upon their reason that they reason away God.
They say God is not a person we can ever see.
They say God is a Spirit. So he is, but he is a person, too, and became a man and walked the earth
once. Scripture tells us very plainly that God has a
dwelling place. There is no doubt whatever about
that. A dwelling place indicates personality. God's
dwelling place is in heaven. He has a dwelling
place, and we are going to be inmates of it. Therefore we shall see Him.

In 1 Kings 8:30, we read:

And hearken thou to the supplication of thy
servant, and of thy people Israel, when they
shall pray toward this place: and hear thou in
heaven thy dwelling place; and when thou
hearest, forgive.

The idea that heaven is everywhere and nowhere is not according to Scripture. Heaven is
God's habitation, and when Christ came on earth

71

He taught us to pray: "Our Father which art in heaven" (Matthew 6:9). This habitation is spoken of as "the city of eternal life." Think of a city without a cemetery—they have no dying there. If there could be such a city as that found on this earth what a rush there would be to it! How men would try to reach that city! You cannot find one on the face of this earth. A city without tears—God wipes away all the tears up yonder. This is a time of weeping, but by and by there will be a time when God shall call us, where there will be no tears. A city without pain, a city without sorrow, without sickness, without death. There is no darkness there. "The Lamb is the light thereof" (Revelation 21:23). It needs no sun, it needs no moon.

The paradise of Eden was as nothing compared with this one. The tempter came into Eden and triumphed, but in that city nothing that defileth shall ever enter. There will be no tempter there. Think of a place where temptation cannot come. Think of a place where we shall be free from sin; where pollution cannot enter and where the righteous shall reign forever. Think of a city that is not built with hands, where the buildings do not grow old with time; a city whose inhabitants are numbered by no census, except the Book of Life, which is the heavenly directory. Think of a city through whose streets runs no tide of business, where no hearses from day to day move slowly with their sad burdens to the cemetery: a city without griefs or graves, without sins or sorrows, without marriages or mournings, without births or burials; a city which glories in having Jesus for its King, angels for its guards, and whose citizens are saints!

We believe this is just as much a place and just as much a city as is New York, London, or Paris. We believe in it a good deal more, because earthly cities will pass away, but this city will remain forever. It has foundations whose builder and maker is God. Some of the grandest cities the world has ever known have not had foundations strong enough to last.

Tyre and Sidon

Take for instance Tyre and Sidon. They were rival cities something like New York and Philadelphia, or St. Louis and Chicago. When the patriarch Jacob gave his sons his blessing, he spoke of Sidon. In the splitting up of Canaan among the tribes of Israel by Joshua, Tyre and Sidon seem to have fallen to the lot of Asher, though the old inhabitants were never fully driven out. We read in Mark: "Jesus withdrew himself with his disciples to the sea: and a great multitude from Galilee followed him, and from Judaea, and from Jerusalem, and from Idumaea, and from beyond Jordan; and they about Tyre and Sidon, a great multitude, when they heard what things He did, came unto Him" (3:7–8). We find in Acts 27:3, that when the ship touched at Sidon, the captain of the guards, who was taking Paul prisoner to appear before Caesar at Rome, let Paul go and visit some of his friends there to refresh himself. From this it has been inferred that at that time there must have been a Christian church there, although the people generally worshiped the Queen of Heaven, who was represented as crowned with the crescent moon.

There are some persons now, you know, who adore a Queen of Heaven. They picture her with the moon beneath her feet. Even the Hebrews, when they saw "the moon walking in brightness," along the clear skies of Palestine, impressed by its beauty, fell into idolatry. In the book of Jeremiah the prophet says:

> The children gather wood, and the fathers kindle the fire, and the women knead their dough, to make cakes to the queen of heaven, and to pour out drink offerings unto other gods. (7:18)

In answer to the prophet's reproof we find them saying, in the forty-fourth chapter, beginning at the sixteenth verse:

> As for the word that thou hast spoken unto us in the name of the Lord, we will not hearken unto thee. But we will certainly do whatsoever thing goeth out of our own mouth, to burn incense unto the queen of heaven, and to pour out drink offerings unto her, as we have done. (44:16)

Is it any wonder that a little farther on we should find addressed to them this language:

> The Lord could no longer bear, because of the evil of your doings, and because of the abominations which ye have committed; therefore is your land a desolation, and an astonishment, and a curse, without an inhabitant, as at this day. (44:22)

In the resurrection they neither marry nor are given in marriage. There will be no "Queen" in heaven.

Tyre is mentioned by Joshua as "a strong city," and both Isaiah and Ezekiel speak of it. In fact, there is a great deal in Scripture about it. Nebuchadnezzar, Alexander the Great, and other kings have fought over it, and hosts of lives have been lost in taking what is now a ruin. Alexander once destroyed it, but it was afterward rebuilt. We find in the inspired Word of God descriptions of what this city once was, from which we can form some idea of its beauty. The whole of the twenty-seventh chapter of Ezekiel is taken up with Tyrus, as it was called then:

> O thou that art situate at the entry of the sea, which art a merchant of the people for many isles, Thus saith the Lord God; O Tyrus, thou hast said, I am of perfect beauty. Thy borders are in the midst of the seas, thy builders have perfected thy beauty. They have made all thy ship boards of fir trees of Senir: they have taken cedars from Lebanon to make masts for thee. (27:3–5)

So it goes on:

> Fine linen with broidered work from Egypt was that which thou spreadest forth to be thy sail; blue and purple from the isles of Elishah was that which covered thee. (v. 7)

A little farther on it says:

Thy riches, and thy fairs, thy merchandise, thy mariners, and thy pilots, thy calkers, and the occupiers of thy merchandise, and all thy men of war, that are in thee, and in all thy company which is in the midst of thee, shall fall into the midst of the seas in the day of thy ruin. . . . Thine heart was lifted up because of thy beauty, thou hast corrupted thy wisdom by reason of the brightness: I will cast thee to the ground, I will lay thee before kings, that they may behold thee. (27:27; 28:17)

The terrible prophecies of its downfall have all been literally fulfilled. We find them in the twenty-sixth chapter of Ezekiel, beginning with the third verse:

Thus saith the Lord God; Behold I am against thee, O Tyrus, and will cause many nations to come up against thee, as the sea causeth his waves to come up. And they shall destroy the walls of Tyrus, and break down her towers: I will also scrape her dust from her, and make her like the top of a rock. It shall be a place for the spreading of nets in the midst of the sea: for I have spoken it, saith the Lord God: and it shall become a spoil to the nations.

Travelers now describe the site of Tyre as "a heap of ruins, broken arches and vaults, tottering walls and towers, with a few starving wretches housed amid the rubbish." A large part of it is underwater, a portion of the ruins a place to spread nets upon, and the rest has become indeed "like the top of a rock."

Thus passes away the glory of the world. This Book tells us of the glory of a city that we no longer see, but which has been. It tells us also of the glory of a greater City that we have not seen, but shall see if we but follow in the way.

O happy harbor of God's saints!
O sweet and pleasant soil!
In thee no sorrow can be found,
Nor grief, nor care, nor toil.
Thy gardens and thy goodly walks
Continually are green,
Where grow such sweet and pleasant flowers
As nowhere else are seen.
No candle needs, no moon to shine,
No glittering star to light,
For Christ, the King of Righteousness,
Forever shineth bright.

Our Names Recorded There

We are told that one time just before sunrise, two men got into a dispute about what part of the heavens the sun would first appear in. They became so excited over it that they began to fight, and beat each other over the head so badly that when the sun arose neither of them could see it. So there are persons who go on disputing about heaven until they dispute themselves out of it, and more who dispute over hell until they dispute themselves into it.

The Hebrews in their writings tell us of three distinct heavens. The air—the atmosphere about the earth—is one heaven; the firmament where the stars are is another, and above that is the heaven of heavens, where God's throne is and the mansions of the Lord are—those mansions of light and peace which are the abode of the blessed, the homes of the Redeemer and the redeemed.

This is the heaven where Christ is. This is the place we read of in Deuteronomy: "Behold the heaven and the heaven of heavens is the Lord's thy God, the earth also, with all that therein is" (10:14).

In 2 Corinthians, Paul, speaking of himself, says:

> I knew a man in Christ above fourteen years ago, (whether in the body, I cannot tell; or whether out of the body, I cannot tell: God knoweth;) such an one caught up to the third heaven. (12:2)

Some people have wondered what the third heaven means. That is where God dwells and where the storms do not come. There sits the incorruptible Judge. Paul, when he was caught up there, heard things that it was not lawful for him to utter, and he saw things that he could not speak of down here. The higher up we get in spiritual matters, the nearer we seem to heaven. There our wishes are fulfilled at last. We may cry out like the psalmist:

> One thing have I desired of the Lord, that will I seek after; that I may dwell in the house of the Lord all the days of my life, to behold the beauty of the Lord, and to inquire in His temple. (27:4)

We are assured by Christ Himself that our names will be written in heaven if we are only His. In the tenth chapter of Luke and the twentieth verse it reads: "Notwithstanding in this rejoice not, that the spirits are subject unto you; but rather rejoice, because your names are written in heaven." A little while before these words were uttered by the Savior, calling together seventy of His disciples, He sent them forth in couples to preach the gospel in the cities of Galilee and Judea.

There are people nowadays who have no faith in revivals. Yet the greatest revival the world ever saw was during the five or six years that John the Baptist and Jesus were preaching, followed by the preaching of the apostles and disciples after Christ left the earth. For years the country was stirred from one end to the other. There were probably men then who stood out against the revival. They might have called it "spasmodic," and refused to believe in it. Perhaps they said, "It is a nine days' wonder and will pass away in a little while, and there will be nothing left of it." No doubt men talked in those days just as they talk now.

All the way down from the time of Christ and His apostles there have been men who have opposed the work of God, and some of them professing to be disciples of the Lord Jesus Christ, all because it has not been done in their way. When the Spirit of God comes, He works in his own way. We must learn the lesson that we are not to mark out any channels for Him to work in, for He will work in His own way when He comes.

These disciples came back after their work. The Spirit had worked with them, and the devils were subject to them, and they had power over disease, and they had power over the Enemy, and they were filled with success. They were probably having a sort of jubilee meeting, and Christ came in and said: "Rejoice not, that the spirits are subject unto you; but rather rejoice, because your names are written in heaven." This brings us face-to-face with the doctrine of assurance.

Assurance

I find a great many people up and down Christendom who do not accept this doctrine. They believe it is impossible for us to know in this life whether we are saved or not. If this be true, how are we going to get over what Christ has said as we find it here recorded? If my name is written in heaven, how can I rejoice over it unless I know it? These men were to rejoice that their names were already there, and the name of each one who is a child of God is there, sent on for registry before.

A party of Americans a few years ago, on their way from London to Liverpool, decided that they would stop at the Northwestern Hotel, but when they arrived they found the place had been full for several days. Greatly disappointed, they took up their baggage and were about starting off, when they noticed a lady of the party preparing to remain.

"Are you not going, too?" they asked.

"Oh no," she said, "I have good rooms all ready."

"Why, how does that happen?"

"Oh," she said, "I telegraphed on ahead, a few days ago."

Now that is what the children of God are doing; they are sending their names on ahead; they are securing places in the mansions of Christ in time. If we are truly children of God our names have gone on before, and there will be places awaiting us at the end of the journey. You know we are only travelers down here. We are away from home. When the [Civil War] was going on, the soldiers on the battlefield, the Southern soldiers and the Northern soldiers, wanted nothing better to live in than tents. They longed for the war to close that they might go home. They cared nothing to have palaces and mansions on the battlefield. Well, there is a terrible battle going on now, and by and by, when the war is over, God will call us home. The tents are good enough for us while journeying through this world. It is only a night, and then the eternal day will dawn.

The Book of Life

Two ladies met on a train not long ago, one of them going to Cairo, Illinois, and the other to New Orleans. Before they reached Cairo they had formed a strong attachment for each other, and the Cairo lady said to the lady who was going to New Orleans:

"I wish you would stay for a few days in Cairo; I would like to entertain you."

"Well," said the other, "I would like to very much, but I have packed up all my things and sent them ahead, and I haven't anything except what I have on, but they are good enough to travel in."

I learned a lesson there. I said, "Almost anything is good enough to travel in, and it is a great deal better to have our joys and comforts ready for us in heaven, waiting until we get there, than to wear them out on our toilsome, trying earthly journey."

Heaven is the place of victory and triumph. This is the battlefield; there is the triumphal procession. This is the land of the sword and the spear; that is the land of the wreath and the crown. Oh, what a thrill of joy will shoot through the hearts of all the blessed when their conquests will be made complete in heaven; when death itself, the last of foes, shall be slain, and Satan dragged as captive at the chariot wheels of Christ! Men may oppose as much as they will this doctrine of assurance; nevertheless it is clearly taught in Scripture.

The Opening of the Books

A great many laugh at the idea of there being books in heaven; but in the twelfth chapter of the prophecy of Daniel, and the first verse, we find:

> And at that time shall Michael stand up, the great prince which standeth for the children of thy people: and there shall be a time of trouble, such as never was since there was a nation even to that same time: and at that time thy people shall be delivered, every one that shall be found written in the book.

There is a terrible time coming upon the earth; darker days than we have ever seen, and they whose names are written in the Book of Life shall be delivered. Then again, in Philippians 4:3, we read:

And I entreat thee also, true yokefellow, help those women which laboured with me in the gospel, with Clement also, and with other of my fellowlabourers, whose names are in the book of life.

Paul, writing to the Christians at Philippi, where he had so much opposition, and where he was cast into jail, says in effect: Just take my regards to the good brethren and sisters who worked with me and whose names are written in the Book of Life. This shows that they taught the doctrine of assurance in the very earliest days of Christianity. Why should we not teach it and believe it now?

Travelers in China told me that the Chinese have in their courts two great books. When a man is tried and found innocent, they write his name down in the book of life. If he is found guilty, they write his name down in the book of death. I believe firmly that every man or woman has his or her name in the Book of Death or the Book of Life. Your name cannot be in both books at the same time. You cannot be in death and in life at the same time, and it is your own privilege to know which it is.

In Revelation 13:8, we read:

And all that dwell upon the earth shall worship him [that is, the Antichrist], whose names are not written in the book of life of the Lamb slain from the foundation of the world.

And again, chapter 20:12:

And I saw the dead, small and great, stand before God; and the books were opened: and another book was opened, which is the book of life: and the dead were judged out of those things which were written in the books, according to their works.

And again, chapter 21:27:

And there shall in no wise enter into it [the Holy City] any thing that defileth, neither whatsoever worketh abomination, or maketh a lie: but they which are written in the Lamb's book of life.

There can be no true peace, there can be no true hope, there can be no true comfort, where there is uncertainty. I am not fit for God's service, I cannot go out and work for God, if I am in doubt about my own salvation.

No Room for Doubt

A mother has a sick child. The child is just hanging between life and death. There is no rest for that mother. You have some friend on a train that is wrecked, and the news comes that twenty have been killed and wounded, and their names are not given; you are in terrible uncertainty, and there is no rest or peace until you know the facts. The reason why there are so many in the churches who will not go out and help others is that they are not sure they have been saved themselves. If I thought I was dying myself, I would be in a poor condition to save anyone else. Before I can pull anyone else out of the water, I must have a firm footing on shore myself. We can have this complete assurance if we will. It does not do to *feel* we are all right, but we must *know* it. We must read our titles *clear* to mansions in the skies; the apostle John says: "Beloved, *now* are we the sons of God." He does not say we are going to be.

People, when asked if they are Christians, give some of the strangest answers you ever heard. Some will say, if you ask them: "Well—well—well, I—I hope I am." Suppose a man should ask me if I am an American. Would I say, "Well I—well I—I hope I am"? I know that I was born in this country, and I know I was born in the Spirit of God more than twenty years ago. All the infidels in the world could not convince me that I have not a different spirit than I had before I became a Christian. "That which is born of the flesh is flesh, and that which is born of the Spirit is spirit," and a man can soon tell whether he is born of the Spirit by the change in his life.

The Spirit of Christ is a spirit of love, joy, peace, humility, and meekness, and we can soon find out whether we have been born of that spirit or not; we are not to be left in uncertainty. Job lived back there in the dark ages, but he *knew*. The dark billows came rolling and surging up against him, but in the midst of the storm you can hear his voice saying: "I *know* that my redeemer liveth" (Job 19:25; italics added). He had something better than a hope.

A man may have his name written in the highest chronicles down here, but the record may be lost; he may have it carved in marble, and still it may perish; some charitable institution may bear his name, and yet he may be soon forgotten; but his name will never be erased from the scrolls that are kept above. Seeking to perpetuate one's name on earth is like writing on the sand by the sea-shore; to be perpetual it must be written on the eternal monuments. It has been said that the way to see our names as they stand written in the Book of Life is by reading the work of sanctification in our own hearts. It needs no miraculous voice from heaven, no extraordinary signs, no unusual feel-ing. We need only find our hearts desiring Christ and hating sin, our minds obedient to the divine commands.

We may be sure that belonging to some church is not going to save us, although every saved man ought to be connected with one. When Daniel died in Babylon, no one had to hunt up an old church record to find out if he was all right. When Paul was beheaded by Nero, no one had to look over the register. On the other hand, no one thinks Pontius Pilate was a saint because his name is in the creed.

They lived so that the world knew what they were. Paul says: "I am persuaded that he is able to keep that which I have committed unto Him against that day" (2 Timothy 1:12). *There* is assur-ance. "Who shall separate us from the love of Christ?" he asks, then gives the answer: "Neither death, nor life, nor angels, nor principalities, nor powers, nor things present, nor things to come" (Romans 8:35, 38). He just challenges them all, but they could not separate him from the love that was in Christ.

It is dishonoring to God to go on hoping—and only hoping—that we "are going" to be saved.

False Professors

Yet there are some who ought *not* to have assurance. It would be an unfortunate thing for any unconverted church member to have assurance. There are some who profess great assurance who ought not to have it—those whose lives do not correspond. This class is represented by the man at the wedding feast who did not have on a wedding garment.

They are like some lilies—fair to see but foul of smell. They are dry shells with no kernel inside. The crusaders of old used to wear a painted cross upon their shoulders. So there are a good many nowadays who take up crosses that sit just as lightly —mere things of ornament—passports to respectability, cheap make-believes, for a struggle that has never been made, and a crown that has never been striven for.

You may very often see dead fish floating with the stream, but you never saw a dead fish swimming against it. Well, that is your false believer; that is the hypocrite. Profession is just floating down the stream, but *con*fession is swimming against it, no matter how strong the tide. The sanctified man and the unsanctified one look at heaven very differently. The unsanctified man simply chooses heaven in preference to hell. He thinks that if he must go to either one he would rather try heaven.

It is like a man with a farm who has a place offered him in another country, where there is said

to be a gold mine. He hates to give up all he has
and take any risk. But if he is going to be banished,
and must leave, and has his choice of living in a
wilderness or digging in a coal pit, or else take the
gold mine, then there is no hesitation.

The unregenerate man likes heaven better
than hell, but he likes this world the best of all.
When death stares him the face, then he thinks he
would like to get to heaven. The true believer
prizes heaven above everything else, and is always
willing to give up the world. Everybody wants to
enjoy heaven after they die, but they don't want to
be heavenly minded while they live. To the Christian it is a sure promise, with no room for doubt,
and there is no reason for hesitation.

The heir to some great estate, while a child,
thinks more of a dollar in his pocket than all his
inheritance. So even some professing Christians
sometimes are more elated by a passing pleasure
than they are by their title to eternal glory. In a
little while we will be there. How glorious is the
thought! Everything is prepared. That is what
Christ went up to heaven for. In a little while we
will be gone. We are:

> Only waiting til the shadows
>   Are a little longer grown,
> Only waiting till the glimmer
>   Of the day's last beam has flown;
> Then from out the gathered darkness,
>   Holy, deathless stars shall rise,
> By whose light our souls shall gladly
>   Tread their pathway to the skies.

HEAVEN
Its Riches

JERUSALEM, MY HOME

Jerusalem, my Home,
Where shines the royal throne;
Each king casts down his golden crown
Before the Lamb thereon.
Thence flows the crystal river,
And flowing on forever,
With leaves and fruits on either hand,
The Tree of Life shall stand.
In blood-washed robes, all white and fair,
The Lamb shall lead His chosen there,
While clouds of incense fill the air—
Jerusalem, my Home!

Jerusalem, my Home!
Where saints in glory reign,
Thy haven safe, O when shall I,
Poor, storm-tossed pilgrim, gain?
At distance dark and dreary,
With sin and sorrow weary,
For thee I toil, for thee I pray,
For thee I long alway.
And lo, mine eyes shall see thee, too;
Oh, rend in twain, thou veil of blue,
And let the Golden City through—
Jerusalem, my Home!

—Hopkins

5

Its Riches

*Lay up for yourselves treasures in heaven . . . :
for where your treasure is, there will your heart
be also.*   Matthew 6:20–21

No man thinks himself rich until he has all he
wants. Very few people are satisfied with earthly
riches. If they want anything at all that they cannot
get, that is a kind of poverty. Sometimes the richer
the man the greater the poverty. Somebody has
said that getting riches brings care; keeping them
brings trouble; abusing them brings guilt; and losing them brings sorrow. It is a great mistake to
make so much of riches as we do. But there are
some riches that we cannot praise too much, that
never pass away. They are the treasures laid up in
heaven for those who truly belong to God.

No matter how rich or elevated we may be
here, there is always something that we want. The
greatest chance the rich have over the poor is the
one they enjoy the least—that of making themselves happy. Worldly riches never make anyone
truly happy. We all know, too, that they often take
wings and fly away. It is said of Midas that whatever he touched turned into gold, but with his long
ears he was not much the better for it.

There is a great deal of truth in some of these old fables. Money, like time, ought not to be wasted, but I pity that man who has more of either than he knows how to use. There is no truer saying than that man by doing good with his money, stamps, as it were, the image of God upon it and makes it pass current for the merchandise of heaven; but all the wealth of the universe would not buy a man's way there. Salvation must be taken as a gift for the asking. There is no man so poor in this world that he may not be a heavenly millionaire.

Gold, a Bad Life Preserver

How many are worshiping gold today! Where war has slain its thousands, gain has slain its millions. Its history in all ages has been the history of slavery and oppression. At this moment what an empire it has! The mine with its drudges, the factory with its misery, the plantation with its toil, the market and exchange with their haggard and care-worn faces—these are but specimens of its menial servants. Titles and honors are its rewards, and thrones are at its disposal. Among its counselors are kings, and many of the great and mighty of the earth are its subjects. This spirit of gain tries even to turn the globe itself into gold.

It is related that Tarpeia, the daughter of the governor of the fortress situated on the Capitoline Hill in Rome, was captivated with the golden bracelets of the Sabine soldiers and agreed to let them into the fortress if they would give her what they wore upon their left arms. The contract was made; the Sabines kept their promise. Tatius, their commander, was the first to deliver this bracelet and shield. The coveted treasures were thrown upon the traitress by each of the soldiers, till she sank beneath their weight and expired. Thus does the weight carry many a man down.

When the steamship "Central America" went down, several hundred miners were on board, returning to their early homes and friends. They had made their fortunes and expected much happiness in enjoying them. In the first of the horror gold lost its attraction to them. The miners took off their treasure belts and threw them aside. Carpet bags full of shining gold dust were emptied on the floor of the cabin. One of them poured out one hundred thousand dollars' worth in the cabin, and bade anyone take it who would. Greed was overpowered, and the gold found no takers. Dear friends, it is well enough to have gold, but sometimes it is a bad life preserver. Sometimes it is a mighty weight that crushes us down to hell.

The Reverend John Newton one day called to visit a family that had suffered the loss of all they possessed by fire. He found the pious mistress and saluted her with: "I give you joy, madam."

Surprised, and ready to be offended, she exclaimed:

"What! Joy that all my property is consumed?"

"Oh, no," he answered, "but joy that you have so much property that fire cannot touch."

This allusion to her real treasures checked her grief and brought reconciliation. As we read in Proverbs 15:6: "In the house of the righteous is much treasure: but in the revenues of the wicked is trouble." I have never seen a dying saint who was rich in heavenly treasures who had any regret; I have never heard such a one say he had lived too much for God and heaven.

Getting Waterlogged

A friend of mine said he was at the River Mersey, in Liverpool, a few years ago, and he saw a vessel which had to be towed with a great deal of care into the harbor. It was clear down to the water's edge and he wondered why it did not sink. Pretty soon there came another vessel, without any help at all; it did not need any tug to tow it in, but it steamed right up the Mersey past the other vessels. He made inquiry, and he found the vessel that had to be towed in was what they called waterlogged—that is, it was loaded with lumber and material of that kind; and having sprung a leak had partially sunk, and it was very hard work to get into the harbor. Now, I believe there are a great many professed Christians, a great many, perhaps, who are really Christians, who have become waterlogged. They have too many earthly treasures, and it takes nearly the whole church—the whole spiritual power of the church—to look after these worldly Christians, to keep them from going back entirely into the world. Why, if the whole church were, as John Wesley said, "hard at it, and always at it," what a power there would be, and how soon we would reach the world and the masses; but we are not reaching the world, because the church itself has become conformed to the world and worldly minded, and because so many are wondering why they do not grow in grace while they have more of the earth in their thoughts than God.

Ministers would not have to urge people to live for heaven if their treasures were up there; they could not help it; their hearts would be there, and if their hearts were there their minds would be up there, and their lives would tend toward heaven. They could not help living for heaven if their treasures were there.

A little girl one day said to her mother: "Mama, my Sunday school teacher tells me that this world is only a place in which God lets us live a while, that we may prepare for a better world. But, mother, I do not see anybody *preparing*. I see you preparing to go into the country, and Aunt Eliza is preparing to come here; but I do not see anyone preparing to go there; why don't they try to get ready?"

A certain gentleman in the South, before the war, had a pious slave, and when the master died they told him he had gone to heaven.

The old slave shook his head, "I's 'fraid Massa no gone there," he said.

"But why, Ben?" he was asked.

"Cos, when Massa go North, or go a journey to the Springs, he talk about it a long time, and get ready. I never hear him talk about going to heaven; never see him get ready to go there!"

So there are a good many who do not get ready. Christ teaches in the Sermon on the Mount:

Lay not up for yourselves treasures upon earth, where moth and rust doth corrupt, and where thieves break through and steal: but lay up for yourselves treasures in heaven, where neither moth nor rust doth corrupt, and where thieves do not break through nor steal: for where your treasure is, there will your heart be also. (Matthew 6:19–21)

Treasures of the Heart

It does not take long to tell where a man's treasure is. In fifteen minutes' conversation with most men you can tell whether their treasures are on the earth or in heaven. Talk to a patriot about his country, and you will see his eyes light up; you will find he has his heart there. Talk to some businessmen, and tell them where they can make a thousand dollars, and see their interest; their hearts are there. You talk to fashionable people who are living just for fashion, of its affairs, and you will see their eyes kindle; they are interested at once; their hearts are there. Talk to a politician about politics, and you see how suddenly he becomes interested. But talk to a child of God, who is laying up treasures in heaven, about heaven and about his future home and see what enthusiasm. "Where your treasure is, there will your heart be also."

Now, it is just as much a command for a man to "lay up treasure in heaven" as it is that he should not steal. Some people think all the commandments are in those ten that were given on Sinai, but when Jesus Christ was here, He gave us many other commandments. There is another commandment in this Sermon on the Mount: "Seek ye first the kingdom of God, and his righteousness; and all these things shall be added unto you" (Matthew 6:33). Here is a command that we are to lay up treasure in heaven and not on earth. The reason there are so many broken hearts in this land, the reason there are so many disappointed people, is because they have been laying up their treasures down here.

The worthlessness of gold, for which so many are striving, is illustrated by a story that Dr. Arnot used to tell. A ship bearing a company of emigrants has been driven from her course and wrecked on a desert island, far from the reach of man. There is no way of escape; but they have a good stock of food. The ocean surrounds them, but they have plenty of seeds, a fine soil, and a genial sun, so there is no danger.

Before the plans are laid, an exploring party discovers a gold mine. There the whole party go to dig. They labor day after day and month after month. They get great heaps of gold. But spring is past, and not a field has been cleared, not a grain of seed put into the ground. The summer comes and their wealth increases; but their stock of food grows small. In the fall they find that their heaps of gold are worthless. Famine stares them in the face. They rush to the woods, they fell trees, dig up the roots, till the ground, sow the seed. It is too late! Winter has come and their seed rots in the ground. They die of want in the midst of their treasures.

This earth is the little isle; eternity the ocean around it; on this shore we have been cast. There is a living seed; but the mines of gold attract us. We spend spring and summer there; winter overtakes us in our toil; we are without the Bread of Life, and we are lost. Let us then who are Christians value all the more the home which holds the treasures that no one can take away. Dr. Muhlenberg, a Lutheran clergyman, has written beautifully:

Who would live alway, away from his God,
Away from yon heaven, that blissful abode;
Where the rivers of pleasure flow o'er the bright plains,
And the harps of gold pour out their glorious strains;
And the saints of all ages in harmony meet
Their Savior, and brethren transported, to greet;
While the anthems of rapture unceasingly roll,
And the smile of the Lord is the feast of the soul?
That heavenly music, what is it I hear?
The notes of the harpers ring sweet on my ear.
To see soft unfolding those portals of gold—
The King, all arrayed in His beauty, behold!
Oh, give me, oh, give me, the wings of a dove,
Let me hasten my flight to those mansions above!
Ay, 'tis now that my soul on swift pinions would soar,
And in ecstasy bid earth adieu evermore.

A Blackboard Lesson

When I was in San Francisco, I went into a
Sabbath school the first Sunday I was there. It was
a rainy day, and there were so few present that the
Superintendent thought of dismissing them, but
instead, he afterward invited me to speak to the
whole school as one class. The lesson was that pas-
sage from the Sermon on the Mount: "Lay not up
for yourselves treasures upon earth, where moth
and rust doth corrupt, and where thieves break
through and steal."

I invited a young man to the blackboard, and
we proceeded to compare a few things that some
people have on earth, and a few things that other
people have in heaven.

"Now," said I, "name some earthly treasure."

They all shouted "Gold."

"Well, that is so," I said; "I suppose that is your greatest treasure out here in California. Now let us go on; what is another?"

A second boy shouted, "Lands."

"Well," I said, "we will put down Lands."

"What else do the people out here in California think a good deal of and have their hearts set on?"

They said, "Houses."

"Put that down. What else?"

"Pleasure."

"Put that down."

"Honor—fame."

"Put that down."

"Business."

"Yes," I said; "a great many people have their hearts buried in their business—put that down." As if a little afraid, one of them said "dress," and the whole school smiled.

"Put that down," I said. "Why, I believe there are some people in the world who think more of dress than any other thing. They just live for dress. I heard not long ago from very good authority, of a young lady who was dying of tuberculosis. She had been living in the world and for the world, and it seemed as if the world had taken full possession of her. She thought she would die Thursday night, and Thursday she wanted them to crimp her hair, so that she would look beautiful in her coffin. But she didn't die Thursday night. She lingered through Friday, and Friday she didn't want them to take her hair down, but to keep it up until she passed away. And the friends said she looked very beautiful in the casket. Just what people wear—the idea of people having their hearts set upon things of that kind!"

"And what else, now?" Well, they were a little ashamed to say it, but one said:

"Rum."

"Yes," I said, "put that down. There is many a man thinks more of the rum bottle than he does of the kingdom of God. He will give up his wife, he will give up his home and his mother, character and reputation forever for the rum bottle. Many a man by his life is crying out, 'Give me rum, and I will give you heaven, and all its glories. I will sell my wife and children. I will make them beggars and paupers. I will degrade and disgrace them for the rum bottle. That is my treasure.'

"'Oh, thou rum bottle! I worship thee,' is the cry of many—they turn their backs on heaven with all its glories for rum. Some of them thought, when that little boy said 'rum,' that he made a mistake, that it was not a treasure, but it is a treasure to thousands." Another one said:

"Fast horses."

Said I, "Put it down. There is many a man who thinks a good deal of fast horses, and he wants to go out and take a fast horse and drive Sunday, and spend his Sabbath in this way." And after we finished and thought everything we could, I said: "Suppose we just take down some of these heavenly treasures.

"And," said I, "what is there now that the Lord wants us to set our hearts and affections on?" And they all said:

"JESUS."

"That is good; we will put Him down first at the head of the list. Now what else?" And they said:

"Angels."

"Put them down. We will have their society when we go to heaven. That is a treasure up there, really. What else?"

"The friends who have died in Christ, who have fallen asleep in Christ."

"Put them down. Death has taken them from us now, but we will be with them by and by. What else?"

"Crowns."

"Yes, we are going to have a crown, a crown of glory, a crown of righteousness, a crown that fadeth not away. What else?"

"The tree of life."

"Yes," I said, "the tree of life. We shall have a right to it. We can go to that tree and pluck its fruit, eat, and live forever. What else?"

"The river of life."

"Yes, we shall walk upon the banks for that clean river."

"Harps," one said.

Another one said, "Palms."

"Yes," I said, "put them down. Those are treasures that we will have there."

"Purity."

"Yes, there will be none but the pure there. White robes, without spot or wrinkle on our garments. A great many find many flaws in our characters down here, but by and by Christ will present us before the Father without spot and without wrinkle, and we shall stand there complete in Him," I said. "Can you think of anything else?" And one of them said:

"A new song."

"Yes, we shall have a new song. It is the song of Moses and the Lamb. I don't know just who wrote it or how, but it will be a glorious song. I suppose the singing we have here on earth will be nothing compared with the songs of that upper world. Do you know the principal thing we are told we are going to do in heaven is singing, and that is why men ought to sing down here. We ought to begin to sing here so that it will not come strange when we get to heaven. I pity the professed Christian who has not a song in his heart—who never 'feels like singing.' It seems to me if we are truly children of God, we will want to sing about it. And so, when we get there, we cannot help shouting out the loud hallelujahs of heaven."

Then I said: "Is there anything else?" Well, they went on. I cannot give you all, because we put down two columns of the heavenly treasures. We stood there a little while and drew the contrast between the earthly and the heavenly treasures. We looked at them a little while, and when we came to put them all down beside Christ, the earthly treasures looked small, after all. What would all this world full of gold be compared with Jesus Christ? You who have Christ, would you like to part with Him for gold? Would you like to give Him up for all the honor the earth can bestow on you for a few months or a few years? Think of Christ! Think of the treasures of heaven. And then think of these earthly treasures that we have our hearts set upon, and that so many of us are living for.

God blessed that lesson upon the blackboard in a marvelous way, for the man who had been writing down the treasures on the board happened to be an unconverted Sunday school teacher, and had gone out there to California to make money; his heart was set upon gold, and he was living for that instead of for God. That was the idol of his heart, and do you know God convicted him at that blackboard, and the first convert that God gave me on the Pacific coast was that man, and he was the last man who shook hands with me when I left San Francisco. He saw how empty the earthly treasures were and how grand and glorious the riches of heaven. Oh, if God would but open your eyes—and I think if you are honest and ask Him to do it He will—He will show you how empty this world is in comparison with what He has in store.

There are a great many people who are wondering why they do not mount up on wings, as it were, and why they do not make some progress in the divine life; why they do not grow more in grace. I think one reason may be they have too many earthly treasures. We need not be rich to have our hearts set on riches.

We need not go in the world more than other people to have our hearts there. I believe the Prodigal Son was in the far country long before he put his feet there. When his heart reached there he was there. There is many a man who does not mingle so much in the world as others do, but his heart is there, and he would be there if he could, and God looks at the heart.

Now, what we need to do is to obey the voice of the Master, and instead of laying up treasures on earth, lay them up in heaven. If we do that, bear in mind, we shall never be disappointed.

It is clear that idolaters are not going to enter the kingdom of God. I may make an idol of my business; I may make an idol of the wife of my bosom; I may make idols of my children. I do not think you need go to heathen countries to find men guilty of idolatry. I think you will find a great many right here who have idols in their hearts. Let us pray that the spirit of God may banish those idols from our hearts, that we may not be guilty of idolatry; that we may worship God in spirit and truth. Anything that comes between me and God is an idol—anything, I don't care what it is. Business is all right in its place, and there is no danger of my loving my family too much if I love God more; but God must have the first place; and if He has not, then the idol is set up.

All Eternity for Rest

Not the least of the riches of heaven will be the satisfaction of those wants of the soul which are so much felt down here but are never found—such as infinite knowledge, perfect peace, and satisfying love. Like a beautiful likeness that has been marred, daubed all over with streaks of black, and is then restored to its original beauty, so the soul is restored to its full beauty of color when it is washed with the blood of Jesus Christ. The senseless image on the canvas cannot be compared, however, in any other way with the living, rational soul.

Could we but see some of our friends who have gone on before us we would very likely feel like falling down before them. The apostle John had seen so many strange things, yet when one of the bright angels stood before him to reveal some of the secrets of heaven, he fell down to worship him. He says in the last chapter of Revelation:

> And I John saw these things, and heard them. And when I had heard and seen, I fell down to worship before the feet of the angel which shewed me these things. Then saith he unto me, See thou do it not: for I am thy fellowservant, and of thy brethren the prophets, and of them which keep the sayings of this book: worship God. (22:8–9)

Among the wants which we have on earth is the thirst for knowledge. Much as sin has weakened man's mental faculties, it has not taken away any of his desire for knowledge. But with all his efforts, with all that he thinks he knows about astronomy, chemistry, and geology, and the rest of the sciences, his knowledge of the secrets of nature is yet limited.

There are very many things we do not know. Thousands of astronomers have lived and died, and the ages of the world have rolled on, and it was only the other day, as it were, that they discovered that the planet Mars had two moons. Perhaps in ages to come some one will find out that they are not moons at all. This is what most of our human knowledge amounts to.

There is not one of our college professors, and many of them have gone nearly everywhere in the world, but is anxious to learn more and more, to find out new things, to make new discoveries. If we were as familiar with all the stars of the firmament as we are with our own earth, still we would not be satisfied.

Not until we are like God can we comprehend the infinite. Even the imperfect glimpses of God that we get by faith only intensify our desire for more. "For now," as Paul says in 1 Corinthians 13:12,

> we see through a glass, darkly; but then face to face: now I know in part; but then shall I know even as also I am known.

The word Paul used, properly translated, is "mirror." Now we see God, as it were, in a looking glass—but then face-to-face.

Suppose we knew nothing of the sun except what we saw of its light reflected from the moon? Would we not wonder about its immense distance, about its dazzling splendor, about its life-giving power? Now all that we see—the sun, the moon, the stars, the ocean, the earth, the flowers, and above all, man—are a grand mirror in which the perfection of God is imperfectly reflected.

Another want that we have is rest. We get tired of toiling. Yet there is no real rest on earth. We find in the fourth chapter of Hebrews, beginning with the ninth verse:

> There remaineth therefore a rest to the people of God. For he that is entered into his rest, he

also hath ceased from his own works, as God did from His. Let us labour therefore to enter into that rest, lest any man fall after the same example of unbelief. (vv. 9–11)

Now, while we all want rest, I think a great many people make a mistake when they think the church is a place of rest; and when they unite with the church they have a false idea about their position in it. There are a great many who come in to rest. The text tells us: "There remaineth therefore a rest for the people of God," but it does not tell us that the church is a place of rest; we have all eternity to rest in. We are to rest by and by; but we are to work here, and when our work is finished, the Lord will call us home to enjoy that rest. There is no use in talking about rest down here in the enemy's country. We cannot rest in this world where God's Son has been crucified and cast out.

I think that a great many people are going to lose their reward just because they have come into the church with the idea that they are to rest there, as if the church was working for the reward, instead of each one building over against his own house, each one using all his influence toward the building up of Christ's kingdom.

In Revelation 14:13, we read:

And I heard a voice from heaven saying unto me, Write, Blessed are the dead which die in the Lord from henceforth: Yea, saith the Spirit, that they may rest from their labours; and their works do follow them.

Now, death may rob us of money. Death may rob us of position. Death may rob us of our friends; but there is one thing death can never do, and that is, rob us of the work that we do for God. That will live on forever. "Their works do follow them." How much are we doing? Anything that we do outside of ourselves, and not with a mean and selfish motive, *that* is going to live. We have the privilege of setting in motion streams of activity that will flow on when we are dead and gone.

It is the privilege of everyone to live more in the future than he does in the present, so that his life will tell in fifty or a hundred years more than it does now.

John Wesley's influence is a thousandfold greater today than it was when he was living. He still lives. He lives in the lives of thousands and hundreds of thousands of his spiritual descendants.

Martin Luther lives more truly today than he did three centuries ago, when he awakened Germany. He only lived one life, and that for a little while. But now, look at the hundreds and thousands and millions of lives that he is living. There are between fifty and sixty millions of people who profess to be followers of the Lord Jesus Christ, as taught by Martin Luther, who bear his name. He is dead in the sight of the world, but his "works do follow him." He still lives.

The voice of John the Baptist is ringing through the world today, although over nineteen hundred years have passed away since Herodias asked for his death. Herod thought when he beheaded him that he was hushing his voice, but it is ringing throughout the earth today. John the Baptist lives, because he lived for God; but he has entered into his rest, and "his works do follow him."

And if they up yonder can see what is going on upon the earth, how much joy they must have to think that they have set these streams in motion, and that this work is going on—being carried on after them.

If a man lives a mean, selfish life, he goes down to the grave, and his name and everything concerning him goes down in the grave with him. If he is ambitious to leave a record behind him, with a selfish motive, his name rots with his body. But if a man gets outside of himself and begins to work for God, his name will live forever. Why, you may go to Scotland today, and you will find the influence of John Knox over every mountain in Scotland. It seems as if you could almost feel the breath of that man's prayer in Scotland today. His influence still lives. "Blessed are the dead which die in the Lord. . . . They may rest from their labours and their works do follow them." Blessed rest in store; we will rest by and by; but we should not waste time talking about rest while we are here.

If I am to wipe a tear from the cheek of that fatherless boy, I must do it down here. It is not said in Scripture that we shall have the privilege of doing that hereafter. If I am going to help up some fallen man who has been overtaken by sin, I must do it here. We are not going to have the privilege of being coworkers with God in the future—but that is our privilege today. We may not have it tomorrow. It may be taken from us tomorrow; but we can enter into the vineyard and do something today before the sun goes down. We can do something now before we go to glory.

Another want that we feel here is love. Heaven is the only place where the conditions of love can be fulfilled. There love is essentially mutual. Everybody loves everybody else. In this world of wickedness and sin it seems impossible for people to be all on a perfect equality. When we meet people who are bright and beautiful and good, we have no difficulty in loving them. All the people of heaven will be like that. There will be no fear of misplaced confidences there. There we shall never be deceived by those we love. When a suspicion of doubt fastens upon anyone who loves, their happiness from that moment is at an end. There will be no suspicion there.

> Beyond these chilling winds and gloomy skies,
>   Beyond death's cloudy portal,
> There is a land where beauty never dies—
>   Where love becomes immortal.

MAIST ONIE DAY

Ye ken, dear bairn, that we maun part,
When death, cauld death, shall bid us start;
But when he'll send his fearfu' dart
    We canna say,
So we'll mak' ready for his dart
    Maist onie day.

We'll keep a'right and guid wi'in,
Our wark will then be free frae sin.
Upright we'll walk through thick and thin,
    Straight on our way.
Deal just wi'a', the prize we'll win
    Maist onie day.

Ye ken ther's Ane, wha's just and wise,
Has said that a' His bairns should rise,
An' soar aboon the lofty skies,
    And there shall stay.
Being well prepared we'll gain the prize
    Maist onie day.

When He wha made a' things just right,
Shall call us hence to realms of light,
Be it morn or noon, or e'en or night,
    We will obey.
We'll be prepared to tak' our flight
    Maist onie day.

Our lamps we'll fill brimfu' o' oil,
Thet's guid and pure, that wadna spoil,
And keep them burning a' the while,
    To light our way.
Our wark bein' done we'll quit the soil,
    Maist onie day.

Timothy Poland

HEAVEN
Its Rewards

NOT HERE! NOT HERE!

Not here! Not here! Not where the sparkling waters
    Fade into mocking sands as we draw near;
Where, in the wilderness, each footstep falters!
    "I shall be satisfied"; but oh, not here!

There *is* a land where every pulse is thrilling
    With rapture earth's sojourners may not know,
Where heaven's repose the weary heart is stilling,
    And peacefully life's storm-tossed currents flow.

"Satisfied! Satisfied!" The spirit's yearning
    For sweet companionship with kindred minds,
The *silent love* that here meets no returning,
    The *inspiration* which no language finds.

"I shall be satisfied." The soul's vague longings
    The aching void which nothing earthly fills!
Oh! What desires upon my soul are thronging
    As I look upward to the heavenly hills.

Thither my weak and weary steps are tending;
    Savior and Lord, with thy frail child abide;
Guide me toward Home, where, all my wanderings ended,
    I then shall see *Thee*, and *"be satisfied."*

                                            —Anonymous

6

Its Rewards

Every man shall receive his own reward according to his own labour. 1 Corinthians 3:8

My reward is with me, to give every man according as his work shall be. Revelation 22:12

If I understand things correctly, whenever you find men or women who are looking to be rewarded here for doing right, they are unqualified to work for God, because if they are looking for the applause of men, looking for reward in this life, it will disqualify them for the service of God, because they are all the while compromising truth.

They are afraid of hurting someone's feelings. They are afraid that someone is going to say something against them, or there will be some newspaper articles written against them. Now we must trample the world under our feet if we are going to get our reward hereafter. If we live for God we must suffer persecution. The kingdom of darkness and the kingdom of light are at war, and have been, and will be as long as Satan is permitted to reign in this world. As long as the kingdom of darkness is permitted to exist, there will be a conflict; and if you want to be popular in the kingdom of God, if you want to be popular in heaven, and get a reward that shall last forever, you will have to be unpopular here.

If you seek the applause of men, you can't have the Lord say "Well done" at the end of the journey. You can't have both. Why? Because this world is at war with God. This idea that the world is getting better all the while is false. The old natural heart is just as much at enmity with God as it was when Cain slew Abel. Sin leaped into the world full grown in Cain. And from the time that Cain was born into the world to the present, man by nature has been at war with God. This world was not established in grace, and we have to fight "the world, the flesh, and the devil"; and if we fight the world, the world won't like us; and if we fight the flesh, the flesh won't like us. We have to mortify the flesh. We have to crucify the old man and put him under. Then, by and by, we will get our reward, and a glorious reward it will be.

We read in Luke 16:15:

And He said unto them, Ye are they which justify yourselves before men; but God knoweth your hearts: for that which is highly esteemed among men is abomination in the sight of God.

We must go right against the current of this world. If the world has nothing to say against us, we can be pretty sure that the Lord Jesus Christ has very little to say for us. There are those who do not like to go against the current of the world. They say they know this and that is wrong, but they do not say a word against it lest it might make them unpopular. If we expect to get the reward we must fight the good fight of faith. For all such, as Paul has said, "There is laid up for me a crown of righteousness, which the Lord, the righteous judge, shall give me at that day" (2 Timothy 4:8).

Fear of Death

How little do we realize the meaning of the word *eternity!* The whole time between the creation of the world and the ending of it would not make a day in eternity. In time, it is like the infinity of space, whose center is everywhere and whose boundary is nowhere. We read in the epistle to the Hebrews:

> Forasmuch then as the children are partakers of flesh and blood, he also himself likewise took part of the same; that through death he might destroy him that had the power of death, that is, the devil; and deliver them who through fear of death were all their lifetime subject to bondage. (2:14–15)

There are a great many of God's professed children who live in continual bondage, in the constant fear of death. I believe that it is dishonoring God. I believe that it is not His will to have one of His children live in fear for one moment. If you know the truth as it is in Christ, there need be no fear, there need be no dread, because death will only hasten you on to glory; and your names are already there.

And then the next thought is for those who are dear to us. I believe that it is not only our privilege to have *our* names written in heaven, but those of the children whom God has given us; and our hearts ought to go right out to them. The promise is not only to us, but to our children. Many a father's and many a mother's heart is burdened with anxiety for the salvation of their children. If your own name is there, let your next aim in life be to get the children whom God has given you, there also.

A mother was dying in one of our eastern cities a few years ago, and she had a large family of children. She died of tuberculosis, and the children were brought in to her one by one as she was sinking. She gave the oldest one her last message and her dying blessing; and as the next one was brought in she put her hand upon its head and gave it her blessing; and then the next one was brought in, and the next, until at last they brought in the little infant. She took it to her bosom and pressed it to her loving heart, and her friends saw that it was hastening her end; that she was excited, and as they went to take the little child from her, she said: "My husband, I charge you to bring all these children home with you." And so God charges us parents to bring our children home with us; not only to have our own names written in heaven, but those of our children also.

An eminent Christian worker in New York told me a story that affected me very much.

A father had a son who had been sick some time, but he did not consider him dangerously ill; until one day he came home to dinner and found his wife weeping, and he asked, "What is the trouble?"

"There has been a great change in our boy since morning," the mother said, "and I am afraid he is dying; I wish you to go in and see him, and, if you think he is, I wish you to tell him so, for I cannot bear to."

The father went in and sat down by the bedside, and he placed his hand upon his son's forehead, and he could feel the cold, damp sweat of death, and knew its cold, icy hand was feeling for the cords of life, and that his boy was soon to be taken away, and he said to him:

"My son, do you know you are dying?"

The little fellow looked up at him and said:

"No; am I? Is this death that I feel stealing over me, Father?"

"Yes, my son, you are dying."

"Will I live the day out?"

"No; you may die at any moment."

He looked up to his father, and he said: "Well, I shall be with Jesus tonight, won't I, Father?"

And the father answered: "Yes, my boy, you will spend tonight with the Savior," and the father turned away to conceal the tears, that the little boy might not see him weep; but he saw the tears, and he said:

"Father, don't you weep for me; when I get to heaven I will go straight to Jesus and tell Him that ever since I can remember you have tried to lead me to Him."

I have three children, and the greatest desire of my heart is that they may be saved; that I may know that their names are written in the Book of Life. I may be taken from them early; I may leave them in this changing world without a father's care; but I would rather have my children say that of me after I am dead and gone, or if they die before me

I would rather they should take that message to the Master—that ever since they can remember I have tried to lead them to the Master—than to have a monument over me reaching to the skies.

We ought not to look upon death as we do. Bishop Heber has written of a dear friend:

Thou art gone to the grave! but we will not deplore thee,
   Though sorrow and darkness encompass the tomb;
Thy Savior has passed through its portals before thee,
   And the lamp of His love is thy guide through the
     gloom.

Thou art gone to the grave! We no longer behold thee,
   Nor tread the rough paths of the world by thy side;
But the wide arms of Mercy are spread to enfold thee,
   And sinners may die, for the Sinless has died.

The roll is being called, and one after another summoned away, but if the names of our loved ones are there, if we know that they are saved, how sweet it is, after they have left us, to think that we shall meet them by and by; that we shall see them in the morn when the night has worn away!

During the war a young man lay on a cot, and they heard him say, "Here, here!" and someone went to his cot and wanted to know what he wanted, and he said, "Hark! Hush, don't you hear them?"

"Hear whom?" was asked.

"They are calling the roll of heaven," he said, and pretty soon he answered, "Here!"—and he was was gone.

If our names are in the Book of Life, by and by when the name is called, we can say with Samuel, "Here am I!" and fly away to meet Him. And if our children are called away early, oh, it is so sweet to think that they died in Christ; that the great Shepherd gathers them in His arms and carries them in His bosom, and that we shall meet them by and by.

Paul, The Christian Hero

The way to get to heaven is to be saved through faith in Jesus Christ.

We get salvation as a gift, but we have to work it out, just as if we got *a gold mine* for a gift.

I do not get a crown by joining the church or renting a pew.

There was Paul. *He* won his crown. He had many a hard fight; he met Satan on many a battlefield, and he overcame him and wore the crown. It would take about ten thousand of the average Christians of this day or any other to make one of Paul. When I read the life of that apostle, I blush for the Christianity of this, my century. It is a weak and sickly thing.

See what he went through. He five times was scourged. The old Roman custom of scourging was to take the prisoner and bind his wrists together and bend him over in a stooping posture, and the Roman soldier would bring the lash, braided with sharp pieces of steel, down upon the bare back of the prisoner and cut him through the skin, so that men sometimes died in the act of being scourged. But Paul says he was scourged five different times. Now if we should get one stripe upon our backs what a whining there would be; there would be forty publishers after us before the sun went down, and they would want to publish our lives, that they could make capital out of them. But Paul says,

"Five times received I forty stripes save one" (2 Corinthians 11:24). That was nothing for him. Take your stand by his side.

"Paul, you have been beaten by these Jews four times, and they are going to give you thirty-nine stripes more; what are you going to do after you get out of the difficulty? What are you going to do about it all?"

"Do?" says he. "I do this one thing—I press toward the mark of the prize of my high calling; I am on my way to get my crown" (see Philippians 3:13–14). He was not going to lose his crown. "Don't think that a few stripes will turn me away; these light afflictions are nothing."

And so they put on thirty-nine more stripes.

He had sprung into the race for Christ, as it were, and was leaping toward heaven. If you will allow me the expression, the devil got his match when he met Paul. He never switched off to a sidetrack. He never sat down to write a letter to defend himself. All the strength that he had he gave to Christ. He never gave a particle to the world nor to himself to defend himself. "This one thing I do," he said, "I am not going to lose the crown." See that no man takes your crown.

"Thrice I was beaten with rods" (2 Corinthians 11:25). Take your stand again beside him.

"Now, Paul, they have beaten you twice, and they are going to beat you again. What are you going to do? Are you going to continue preaching? If you are, let me give you a little advice. Now, don't be quite so radical; be a little more conservative; just use a little finer language, and, so to speak, cover up the cross with beautiful words and flowery sentences, and tell men that they are pretty good after all, that they are not so bad; and try and pacify the Jews; make friends with them, and get in with the world, and the world will think more of you. Don't be so earnest; don't be so radical, Paul; now come, take our advice. What are you going to do?"

"Do?" he says, "I do this one thing—I press toward the mark of the prize of the high calling." So they put on the rods, and every blow lifts him nearer to God.

Take your stand with him again. They begin to stone him. That is the way they killed those who did not preach to suit them.

It seems as if he was about to be paid back in his own coin, for when Stephen was stoned to death, Paul, then known as Saul, cheered on the crowd.

"Now, Paul, this is growing serious; hadn't you better take back some of the things you have said about Jesus? What are you going to do?"

"Do?" he says, "if they take my life I will only get my crown the sooner."

He would not budge an inch. He had something that the world could not give; he had something it could not take away; he had eternal life, and he had in store a crown of glory.

These Light Afflictions

Three times was he shipwrecked; a night and a day he was in the deep (see 2 Corinthians 11:25). Look at that mighty apostle, a whole night and day in the deep. There he was—shipwrecked, and for what? Was it to make money? He was not after

money. He was just going from city to city, and
town to town, to preach the glorious Gospel of Jesus Christ, and to lift up the cross wherever he had
opportunity.

He went down to Corinth and preached eigh-
teen months, and he didn't have a lot of the leading ministers of Corinth to come on the platform
and sit by his side when he preached. There was
not a man who stood by him. When he reached
Corinth he had none of the leading businessmen
to stand by him and advise him; but the little tentmaker arrives in Corinth a perfect stranger, and
the first thing he does is to find a place where he
can make a tent; he does not go to a hotel. His
means will not allow it; he goes where he can make
his bread by the sweat of his brow. Think of that
great apostle making a tent, and then getting on
the corner of a street and preaching, and perhaps
once in a while he would get into a synagogue, but
the Jews would turn him out. They did not want to
hear him preach anything about Jesus the Crucified.

When I read of the life of such a man, how I
blush to think how sickly and dwarfed Christianity
is at the present time, and how many hundreds
there are who never think of working for the Son
of God and honoring Christ.

Yet when he wrote that letter back to Corinth,
we find him taking an inventory of some things he
had. He is rich, he says, "In journeyings often, in
perils of waters, in perils of robbers, in perils by my
own countrymen, in perils by the heathen, in perils
in the city, in perils in the wilderness, in perils in
the sea, in perils among false brethren" (2 Corin-

thians 11:26–27). This last must have been the hardest of all. "In weariness and painfulness, in watchings often, in hunger and thirst, in fastings often, in cold, in nakedness. Beside those things that are without, that which cometh upon me daily, the care of all the churches" (v. 28).

These are only some of the things that he summed up. Do you know what made him so exceedingly happy? It was because he believed the Scripture; he believed the Sermon on the Mount. We profess to believe it; we pretend to believe it; but few of us more than half believe it. Listen to one sentence in that sermon: "Rejoice, and be exceeding glad: for great is your reward in heaven" when you are persecuted (Matthew 5:12). Now persecution was about all that Paul had.

That was his capital, and he had a good deal of it; he had laid by a good many persecutions, and he was to get a great reward. Christ says: "Rejoice and be exceeding glad, for great is your reward in heaven." If Jesus Christ spoke of it as "great" it must be indeed wonderful. We call things great that may look very small to Jesus Christ; and things that look very small to us may look very large to Him. When the great Christ, the Creator of heaven and earth, He who formed the heavens and the earth by His mighty power, when *He* calls it a great reward, what must it be?

Perhaps some people said to the apostle to the Gentiles: "Now, Paul, you are meeting with too much opposition; you are suffering too much."

Hear him reply: "Our light affliction, which is but for a moment, worketh for us a far more exceeding and eternal weight of glory" (2 Corinthians 4:17).

"Our light affliction," he calls it. We would have called it pretty hard, pretty heavy, would we not?

But he says: "These light afflictions are nothing; think of the glory before me, and think of the crowning time; think of the reward that is laid up for me. I am on my way; the Righteous Judge will give it to me when the time comes"; and that is what filled his soul with joy; it was the thought of reward that the Lord had in store for him.

Now, my friends, let us just for a minute think of what Paul accomplished. Think of going out, as it were, among the heathen; the first missionary to preach to these men, who were so full of wickedness, so full of enmity and bitterness, the glorious Gospel of Jesus Christ, and to tell them that the man who died outside the walls of the city of Jerusalem died the death of a common prisoner—a common felon, in the sight of the world—was the promised Christ; to tell them that they had to believe in that crucified Man in order to enter the kingdom of God. Think of the dark mountain that rose up before him; think of the opposition; think of the bitter persecution—and then think of the trifles in our way.

Songs in Prison

But a great many worldly people think Paul's life was a failure. Probably his enemies, when they put him in prison, thought that would silence him. But do you know that I believe today Paul thanks God more for prisons, for stripes, for the persecution and opposition that he suffered, than for anything else that happened to him here?

The very things we do not like are sometimes the very best for us.

Christians probably might not have these glorious epistles if Paul had not been thrown into prison. There he took up his pen and wrote letters to the Christians in Galatia, Ephesus, Philippi, Colossae, and to Philemon and Timothy. Look at the two epistles that he wrote to the Corinthians. How much has been done for the world by these epistles! What a blessing they have been to the church of God: how great a light they have thrown on man's life! But we might not have had those epistles if it had not been for persecution.

Perhaps John Bunyan blesses God more today for Bedford jail than anything that happened to him. Probably we would not have the *Pilgrim's Progress* if he had not been thrown into that prison. Satan thought he accomplished a great deal when he shut up Bunyan for twelve years and six months; but what a blessing it was to the world! I believe Paul blesses God today for the Philippian jail, and for the imprisonment he suffered in Rome, because it gave him time to write those blessed letters. Talk of Alexander making the world tremble with the tread of his armies, and of Caesar's and Napoleon's power! But here is a little tentmaker, who, without an army, turned the world upside down!

Why?

Because God Almighty was with him.

Paul says in one place: "None of these things move me" (Acts 20:24). They threw him in prison,

but it was all the same; it did not move him. When
he was at Corinth and Athens preaching, it made
no difference. He just "pressed toward the mark
for the prize of the high calling of God in Christ
Jesus" (see Philippians 3:14). If God wanted him to
go through prisons to win the prize, it was all the
same to him. They put him in prison, but they put
the Almighty in with him, and Paul was so linked
to Jesus that they could not separate them. He
would rather be in prison with Christ than out of
prison without Him. He would a thousand times
rather be cast into prison with the Son of God and
suffer a little persecution for a few days here, than
to be living at ease without Him.

He heard the cry, "Come over unto Macedo-
nia, and help us" (Acts 16:9). He went over and
preached, and the first thing that happened to him
was that he was put into the Philippian jail (Acts
16:12–23). Now, if he had been as fainthearted as
most of us, he would have been disappointed and
cast down. There would have been a great com-
plaint.

He would have said: "This is a strange provi-
dence; whatever brought me here? I thought the
Lord called me here; yet here I am in prison in a
strange city. How did I ever get here? How will I
ever get out of this place? I have no money; I have
no friends; I have no attorney; I have no one to
intercede for me, and here I am."

Paul and Silas were not only in prison, but
their feet were made fast in the stocks. There they
were, in the inner prison, a dark, cold, damp dun-
geon. But at midnight the other prisoners heard a
strange sound. They had never heard anything

like it before. They heard singing. I do not know what song those two imprisoned evangelists sang, but I know one thing, it was not "a doleful sound from the tombs." You know we have a hymn, "Hark, from the tombs a doleful sound." They did not sing that, but the Bible tells us they sang praises. That was a queer place to sing praises, was it not?

I suppose it was time for the evening prayers, and that they had just had their evening prayer and then sang their evening hymn. And God answered their prayers, and the old prison shook, and the chains dropped, and the prison doors were opened. Yes, yes; I have no doubt that in glory he thanks God that he went to jail and that the Philippian jailer became converted (Acts 16:24–34).

Swept into Glory

But look at him at Rome. Nero has signed his death warrant. Take your stand and look at the little man. He is small; in the sight of the world he is contemptible (2 Corinthians 12:10); the world frowns upon him. Go to the palace of the king and talk about that criminal—about Paul—and you will see a sneer on their countenances.

"Oh, he is a fanatic," they say; "he has gone mad." I wish the world was filled with such fanatics. I tell you what we want today is a few fanatics like him; men who fear nothing but sin and love no one but God.

Rome never had such a conqueror within her walls. Rome never had such a mighty man as Paul within her boundaries. Although the world looked down upon him—and perhaps he looked very small and contemptible—yet in the sight of heaven he was the mightiest man who ever trod the streets of Rome. Probably there will never be another one like him traveling those streets. The Son of God walked with him, and the form of the Fourth was with him. But go into that prison; there he is. Officials come to him and tell him that Nero has signed his death warrant. He does not tremble; he is not afraid.

"Paul, are you not sorry you have been so zealous for Christ? It is going to cost you your life; if you had to live it over again, would you give it to Jesus of Nazareth?" What do you think the old warrior would reply?

See that eye light up as he says: "If I had ten thousand lives I should give every one of those lives to Christ, and the only regret I have is that I did not commence earlier and serve Him better; the only regret I have now is that I ever lifted my voice against Jesus of Nazareth."

"But they are going to behead you."

"Well, they may take my head, but the Lord has my heart. I care nothing about my head; the Lord has my heart and has had it for years. They cannot separate me from the Lord, and when my head is taken off, I shall depart to be with Christ, which is far better."

And they led him out. I do not know at what hour; perhaps it was early in the morning. There is a tradition tells us that they led him two miles out of the city. Look at the little tentmaker as he goes through the streets of Rome with a firm tread. Look at that giant as he moves through the streets. He is on his way to execution. Take your stand by his side and hear him talk. He is talking of the glory beyond.

He says: "Henceforth there is laid up for me a crown of righteousness. I shall see the King in His beauty tonight. I have longed to be with Him; I have longed to see Him. this is the day of my crowning."

The world scoffed at him, but he did not heed its scoffing. he had something the world had not; burning within him he had a love and zeal which the world knew nothing about. Ah, the love that Paul had for Jesus Christ! But, oh, the greater love the Lord Jesus had for Paul!

The hour has come. The way they used to behead them in those days was for the prisoner to bend his head. Then a Roman soldier took a sword and cut it off. The hour had come, and I seem to see Paul, with a joyful countenance, bending his blessed head, as the soldier's sword comes down and sets his spirit free.

If our eyes could look as Elisha's looked, we might have seen him leap into a chariot of light like Elijah; we would have seen him so sweeping through limitless space.

Look at him now as he mounts higher and higher; look at him, see him move up; up—up—up—ever upward.

Look at him yonder!

See! He is entering now the Eternal City of the glorified saints, the blissful abode of the Savior's redeemed. The prize he so long has sought is at hand. See the gates yonder; how they fly wide open. See the herald angels on the shining battlements of heaven. Hear the glad shout that is passed along, "He is coming! He is coming!" And he goes sweeping through the pearly gates, along the shining way, to the very throne of God, and Christ stands there and says: "Well done, thou good and faithful servant; enter thou into the joy of thy Lord."

Just think of hearing the Master say it! Will not that be enough for everything?

Oh, friends, your turn and mine will come by and by, if we are but faithful. Let us see that we do not lose the crown. Let us awake and put on the whole armor of God; let us press into the conflict; it is a glorious privilege; and then to us too, as to the glorified of old, will come that blessed welcome from our glorified Lord: "Well done, thou good and faithful servant."